The Florida Small Business Legal Handbook:

Starting and Operating a Business

Nikollasa Achli

Dedication

This book is dedicated to all the aspiring entrepreneurs and small business owners in Florida who have the courage to pursue their dreams and make them a reality. Your dedication, resilience, and unwavering spirit inspire us all.

To my family and loved ones, thank you for your endless support, encouragement, and understanding throughout this journey. Your love and belief in me have been invaluable.

To the countless mentors, advisors, and professionals who have shared their expertise and guided me along the way, I am forever grateful for your wisdom and guidance.

And to every small business owner who strives to make a positive impact on their community and the world, may this book serve as a helpful resource to navigate the legal complexities and challenges of starting and operating a business in Florida.

This book is for you.

Acknowledgments

I would like to express my heartfelt gratitude to everyone who contributed to the creation of this book. Their support, guidance, and encouragement were instrumental in bringing this project to fruition.

First and foremost, I want to thank my family and friends for their unwavering support and understanding throughout the writing process. Your love, patience, and belief in me kept me motivated and inspired.

I extend my deepest appreciation to the team at Achli Publishing for their invaluable assistance and expertise. Their dedication to producing high-quality content and their commitment to helping authors succeed are truly commendable.

I am indebted to the legal professionals and experts in the field of small business law who generously shared their knowledge and insights. Your expertise and willingness to educate others have greatly enriched the content of this book.

A special mention goes to the readers and reviewers who provided feedback and constructive criticism. Your input helped shape this book into a more comprehensive and user-friendly resource.

Lastly, I want to acknowledge the countless entrepreneurs and small business owners who have faced challenges, setbacks, and triumphs on their entrepreneurial journeys. Your stories and experiences have served as a constant reminder of the importance and impact of small businesses in our communities.

Thank you all for being a part of this project. Your contributions have made this book possible.

"Success in business requires resilience, determination, and an unwavering belief in your vision. Never give up, for in the face of challenges lie the greatest opportunities." - Richard Branson

Prologue

In the vast landscape of entrepreneurial dreams, where ideas ignite and aspirations take flight, there lies a unique realm known as the small business world. It is a world brimming with ambition, innovation, and the pursuit of success. Within this world, we find ourselves in the vibrant state of Florida, a hub of entrepreneurial opportunities and limitless potential.

"The Florida Small Business Legal Handbook: Starting and Operating a Business" serves as a guidebook, a compass, and a trusted companion for those venturing into the realm of small business ownership in the Sunshine State. Written by an expert attorney, this handbook is designed to equip aspiring entrepreneurs and existing small business owners with the knowledge and tools needed to navigate the legal landscape, make informed decisions, and overcome the challenges that lie ahead.

Within the pages of this handbook, you will embark on a comprehensive exploration of the legal aspects involved in starting and operating a small business in Florida. From choosing a business name to registering trademarks, understanding employment laws to drafting contracts, managing finances to ensuring ethical practices, each chapter is a treasure trove of insights and expert advice.

As you immerse yourself in the knowledge shared, remember that this handbook is more than just words on a page. It is a roadmap, carefully crafted to help you navigate the twists and turns of the small business journey. It is a companion, offering guidance and support when uncertainties arise. It is a source of empowerment, arming you with the tools and information necessary to confidently build and grow your business.

In the pursuit of entrepreneurial dreams, challenges are bound to arise. Legal complexities, financial hurdles, marketing intricacies, and ethical considerations can often seem overwhelming. But fear not, for this handbook is your beacon of knowledge, illuminating the path to success. With each turn of the page, you will gain the insights and understanding needed to overcome obstacles and thrive in the competitive business landscape.

Remember, you are not alone on this journey. Countless entrepreneurs have walked this path before you, and their wisdom and experiences have been distilled within the pages of this handbook. Engage with fellow small business owners, seek mentorship, and tap into the resources and support systems available in Florida's vibrant small business community.

As you embark on this transformative journey of entrepreneurship, may the knowledge gained from "The Florida Small Business Legal Handbook: Starting and Operating a Business" empower you to dream big, take bold steps, and build a thriving business that leaves a lasting impact. May your journey be filled with resilience, creativity, and a deep sense of fulfillment.

Welcome to the small business world in the Sunshine State, where dreams become reality, and possibilities are limitless.

Nikollasa Achli

Author - *The Florida Small Business Legal Handbook: Starting and Operating a Business*

Chapter 1:

Introduction to Starting a Small Business in Florida

Starting a small business in Florida offers numerous opportunities for entrepreneurs to thrive in a vibrant and diverse economy. This chapter serves as an introduction to the key considerations and steps involved in launching your own business venture in the Sunshine State.

Choosing the right legal structure:

Selecting the appropriate legal structure for your business is indeed a critical decision that can significantly impact your business's liability, taxation, and management. There are several options to consider, each with its own advantages and disadvantages.

Sole Proprietorship:

A sole proprietorship is indeed the most straightforward and uncomplicated form of business structure. It offers several advantages, such as complete control over the business and the ability to retain all profits generated. As the sole proprietor, you have the freedom to make decisions independently and shape the direction of the business according to your vision.

One key aspect to consider is the unlimited personal liability associated with a sole proprietorship. In this structure, the business and the owner are considered one and the same in the eyes of the law. This means that you, as the owner, are personally responsible for any debts, liabilities, or legal obligations incurred by the business. In the event of financial difficulties or legal claims against the business, your personal assets may be at risk.

It is important to note that the level of personal liability can vary depending on the nature of the business. Small businesses with low-risk activities, such as consulting services or freelance work, may face fewer potential liabilities compared to businesses involved in high-risk activities, such as manufacturing or construction.

When considering a sole proprietorship, it is crucial to assess the level of risk associated with your business operations and evaluate your personal risk tolerance. If your business involves significant liabilities or potential legal risks, you may want to consider alternative business structures that offer limited liability protection, such as forming a limited liability company (LLC) or incorporating as a corporation.

However, for small businesses with low-risk activities and where personal liability is manageable, a sole proprietorship can be a suitable choice. It offers simplicity, autonomy, and the ability to retain full control over your business and its profits. It is important to consult with an attorney or business advisor to evaluate the specific circumstances of your business and determine the most appropriate legal structure that aligns with your goals and risk management strategy.

Partnership:

Partnerships are a common business structure that allows two or more individuals to combine their resources, expertise, and efforts to operate a business together. There are two main types of partnerships: general partnerships and limited partnerships. Let's explore each type in more detail:

1. General Partnership:

- In a general partnership, all partners share equal rights and responsibilities in the management and operation of the business.
- Each partner contributes to the business's operations, decision-making, and financial obligations.
- General partners have unlimited personal liability for the partnership's debts and obligations. This means that their personal assets may be at risk in the event of legal claims or financial difficulties faced by the partnership.
- General partners are also personally responsible for the actions and liabilities of other partners within the scope of the partnership's business.

2. Limited Partnership:

- A limited partnership consists of two types of partners: general partners and limited partners.
- General partners have similar rights and responsibilities as in a general partnership. They actively manage the business and have unlimited personal liability.
- Limited partners, on the other hand, are passive investors who contribute capital to the business but do not actively participate in its management.
- Limited partners have limited personal liability, meaning their liability is generally limited to the amount of capital they have invested in the partnership.

- Limited partners typically have no control over the day-to-day operations and decision-making of the partnership. Their involvement is limited to their investment in the business.

When considering a partnership as a business structure, it is crucial to understand the implications of each type. General partnerships offer shared decision-making but come with unlimited personal liability for all partners. Limited partnerships provide the opportunity for passive investment but still require general partners to assume unlimited personal liability.

It is essential to consult with an attorney experienced in partnership law to draft a comprehensive partnership agreement that clearly outlines the rights, responsibilities, and liability of each partner. This agreement can help establish a solid foundation for the partnership and mitigate potential disputes or challenges in the future.

By understanding the differences between general partnerships and limited partnerships, individuals can make informed decisions regarding the appropriate business structure for their specific needs and circumstances.

General Partnerships:

In a general partnership, it is crucial to understand the implications of unlimited personal liability. Each partner is personally responsible for the partnership's debts and legal obligations, regardless of whether they were directly involved in incurring them. This means that creditors can pursue the personal assets of each partner to satisfy the partnership's liabilities.

It is important to note that personal liability extends to both contractual and tortious claims. If the partnership fails to fulfill its contractual obligations or is held liable for any damages caused to others, the partners may be personally liable for the resulting losses.

To protect themselves, partners should carefully consider the potential risks and take appropriate measures. Here are a few strategies to mitigate personal liability in a general partnership:

Partnership Agreement: Drafting a comprehensive partnership agreement is indeed a critical step in establishing a clear understanding among partners and mitigating potential disputes or challenges in the future. Here are key components that should be included in a partnership agreement:

1. Introduction and Purpose: Begin the agreement with a clear statement of the partnership's name, purpose, and duration. Define the scope of the partnership's activities and outline its goals and objectives.
2. Contributions and Ownership: Specify the contributions made by each partner, whether in the form of capital, assets, or expertise. Determine the ownership percentages or profit-sharing ratios based on these contributions.
3. Rights and Responsibilities: Clearly define the rights and responsibilities of each partner. This includes decision-making authority, management responsibilities, and roles within the partnership. Address any limitations or restrictions on partners' actions, such as entering into contracts or incurring debts on behalf of the partnership.
4. Allocation of Profits and Losses: Determine how profits and losses will be allocated among the partners. This can be based on the agreed-upon ownership percentages or a different arrangement as specified in the partnership agreement.
5. Personal Liability: Include provisions that limit or allocate personal liability among the partners. This can outline the extent to which partners are personally responsible for the partnership's debts and obligations, ensuring clarity and fairness in sharing liabilities.
6. Dispute Resolution: Establish procedures for resolving disputes among partners, such as mediation or arbitration. Define the process for addressing disagreements, breaches of the agreement, or other conflicts that may arise during the partnership's operation.
7. Partnership Dissolution: Outline procedures for dissolving the partnership, including the circumstances under which dissolution can occur, such as the retirement, resignation, or death of a partner. Specify how assets and liabilities will be distributed upon dissolution.
8. Non-Compete and Non-Disclosure Agreements: Consider including provisions that restrict partners from engaging in competing activities or disclosing sensitive information during and after the partnership's existence to protect the partnership's interests.
9. Succession Planning: Address the process for admitting new partners or transferring ownership interests in the event of a partner's departure, retirement, or death. Define the criteria

and procedures for admitting new partners, including buy-sell provisions or the right of first refusal.

10. Governing Law and Jurisdiction: Specify the governing law and jurisdiction that will govern the partnership agreement, ensuring clarity in legal matters and providing a framework for resolving any legal disputes.

It is essential to consult with an attorney experienced in partnership law to draft a partnership agreement tailored to the specific needs and goals of the partners. The agreement should accurately reflect the intentions and expectations of all parties involved, promoting a clear understanding of rights, responsibilities, and liabilities.

Insurance: Obtaining adequate insurance coverage is indeed a crucial step in protecting partners from potential risks and liabilities. Here are some key types of insurance coverage that partners should consider:

1. General Liability Insurance: This insurance provides coverage for claims related to bodily injury, property damage, or personal injury that may arise from the partnership's operations. It helps protect partners from potential legal costs and damages resulting from accidents or incidents that occur on the partnership's premises or as a result of its activities.

2. Professional Liability Insurance: Also known as errors and omissions (E&O) insurance, professional liability insurance is specifically designed for businesses that provide professional services or advice. It provides coverage for claims arising from alleged negligence, errors, or omissions in the performance of professional duties. This type of insurance is particularly relevant for partnerships that offer professional services, such as law firms, accounting firms, or consulting firms.

3. Product Liability Insurance: If the partnership manufactures, distributes, or sells products, product liability insurance is essential. It provides coverage for claims arising from injuries or damages caused by a defective product. Product liability insurance helps protect partners from potential lawsuits and associated costs.

4. Cyber Liability Insurance: In today's digital age, cyber threats are a significant concern for businesses. Cyber liability insurance provides coverage for expenses related to data breaches, cyberattacks, and the resulting legal liabilities. It

helps protect partners from potential financial losses and damages resulting from cyber incidents.

5. Workers' Compensation Insurance: If the partnership has employees, workers' compensation insurance is typically required by law. It provides coverage for medical expenses, lost wages, and rehabilitation costs for employees who suffer work-related injuries or illnesses. Workers' compensation insurance helps protect partners from potential legal and financial consequences of workplace injuries or accidents.

It is important for partners to carefully evaluate their specific business activities and risks to determine the most appropriate insurance coverage for their partnership. Consulting with an insurance professional experienced in commercial insurance can help partners assess their insurance needs, identify potential gaps in coverage, and obtain the right policies to protect their interests.

Remember, insurance coverage should be regularly reviewed and updated as the partnership evolves and new risks arise. By proactively managing insurance coverage, partners can mitigate potential financial losses and safeguard their partnership against unforeseen events and liabilities..

Asset Protection: Partners in a general partnership may explore structuring their personal assets to provide some level of protection. This can involve transferring assets to legal entities that offer a degree of asset protection, such as trusts or limited liability companies (LLCs). It is important to note that asset protection strategies can vary based on individual circumstances and the laws of the jurisdiction.

Here are two common methods that partners may consider:

1. Trusts: Partners can transfer personal assets into trusts, such as revocable living trusts or irrevocable trusts. Trusts can provide a level of protection by separating the assets from personal ownership. In the event of legal claims or financial difficulties faced by the partnership, assets held in a properly structured trust may be shielded from potential liabilities.

2. Limited Liability Companies (LLCs): Partners may establish an LLC as a separate legal entity to hold personal assets. By doing so, the partners can limit their personal liability to the extent of their investment in the LLC. This means that their personal assets are generally protected from the partnership's debts and obligations.

It is important to consult with a qualified attorney experienced in asset protection and partnership law to explore the most suitable strategies for your specific situation. They can provide personalized advice, help structure the legal entities properly, and ensure compliance with applicable laws and regulations.

However, it is worth noting that asset protection strategies have limitations, and they should not be used to engage in fraudulent activities or evade legitimate obligations. It is crucial to seek professional advice and carefully follow legal and ethical guidelines when implementing asset protection measures.

Remember that asset protection should be just one aspect of a comprehensive risk management strategy. Partners should also focus on maintaining proper insurance coverage, adhering to legal and regulatory requirements, and conducting business in an ethical and responsible manner.

By taking appropriate measures to protect personal assets, partners can potentially minimize their exposure to personal liability in the context of a general partnership. However, it is essential to consult with a qualified professional to ensure that the chosen strategies are suitable for your specific circumstances and comply with applicable laws.

Due Diligence: Conducting thorough due diligence is crucial before entering into any business contracts or agreements on behalf of the partnership. Here are some key considerations to keep in mind during the due diligence process:

1. Review Contract Terms: Carefully review all terms and conditions of the contract, including pricing, payment terms, delivery schedules, and performance expectations. Ensure that the contract accurately reflects the partnership's understanding and expectations.

2. Identify Potential Risks: Identify and assess potential risks associated with the contract, such as financial obligations, performance obligations, intellectual property rights, and termination provisions. Evaluate the impact of these risks on the partnership and consider including appropriate provisions to mitigate or allocate these risks.

3. Legal Compliance: Ensure that the contract complies with all applicable laws, regulations, and industry standards. This includes compliance with federal, state, and local laws

governing the partnership's activities, such as employment laws, environmental regulations, and consumer protection laws.

4. Assess Counterparty's Reputation and Financial Stability: Conduct background research on the counterparty to assess their reputation, financial stability, and track record. Review their business history, financial statements, references, and online presence to ensure they are reliable and capable of fulfilling their contractual obligations.

5. Seek Professional Advice: Consider engaging an attorney experienced in contract law to review the contract and provide guidance. An attorney can help identify potential pitfalls, negotiate favorable terms, and ensure that the contract protects the partnership's interests.

6. Confidentiality and Non-Disclosure: If the contract involves the exchange of sensitive or proprietary information, consider including confidentiality and non-disclosure provisions to protect the partnership's intellectual property and confidential information.

7. Dispute Resolution Mechanisms: Include provisions for dispute resolution, such as mediation or arbitration, to provide a structured and efficient process for resolving conflicts that may arise under the contract. This can help avoid costly and time-consuming litigation.

8. Termination and Exit Clauses: Clearly define the circumstances under which either party can terminate the contract and the associated rights and obligations. Establish procedures for terminating the contract and outline any consequences or remedies in the event of termination.

9. Compliance Monitoring: Establish mechanisms to monitor compliance with the contract, such as reporting requirements, performance metrics, and periodic reviews. This helps ensure that both parties fulfill their obligations and enables timely identification and resolution of any issues.

10. Record-Keeping: Maintain accurate records of all contracts and agreements, including copies of signed contracts, correspondence, and any amendments or modifications. This documentation serves as evidence of the partnership's rights and obligations and can be valuable in the event of disputes or legal challenges.

By conducting thorough due diligence and carefully reviewing and negotiating contract terms, partners can protect the interests of the partnership and minimize potential liabilities. It is advisable to consult with an attorney experienced in contract law to ensure that the partnership's contracts are legally sound and tailored to its specific needs.

Separate Business Finances: Maintaining clear separation between personal and partnership finances is essential for legal and financial purposes. Here are some key steps to ensure proper separation:

1. Establish a Separate Bank Account: Open a dedicated bank account in the name of the partnership. Use this account exclusively for all partnership-related financial transactions, including income, expenses, and payments. Avoid using personal accounts for partnership activities to maintain clear separation.
2. Keep Detailed Financial Records: Maintain accurate and organized financial records for the partnership. This includes invoices, receipts, bank statements, and any other documentation related to income and expenses. Proper record-keeping helps track and document partnership transactions and ensures transparency.
3. Avoid Commingling Funds: Do not mix personal funds with partnership funds. Avoid using personal funds to cover partnership expenses or vice versa. Keeping personal and partnership funds separate reinforces the legal distinction between personal and partnership liabilities and facilitates accurate accounting and reporting.
4. Clearly Document Transactions: Ensure that all financial transactions between the partner(s) and the partnership are appropriately documented. This includes loans, capital contributions, or any other financial transactions. Maintain proper records and agreements to establish the nature and purpose of these transactions.
5. Pay Yourself a Salary or Draw: If partners are entitled to receive compensation from the partnership, establish a clear system for paying yourself a salary or draw. Treat these payments as legitimate business expenses and ensure they are properly recorded in the partnership's financial statements.
6. Consult with an Accountant or Bookkeeper: Seek professional advice from an accountant or bookkeeper experienced in small

business finances. They can provide guidance on proper accounting practices, financial reporting, and maintaining separation between personal and partnership finances.

7. Consult with an Attorney: Consider consulting with an attorney specializing in business and partnership law. They can provide legal advice on maintaining separation, complying with legal requirements, and protecting personal assets from partnership liabilities.

By establishing a clear separation between personal and partnership finances, partners can ensure legal compliance, facilitate accurate financial reporting, and protect personal assets from potential partnership liabilities. It is advisable to maintain proper financial records and consult with professionals to ensure compliance with relevant laws and regulations.

Ongoing Communication: Maintaining open and transparent communication among partners is essential for the success and sustainability of the partnership. Here are some key considerations to foster effective communication:

1. Regular Partner Meetings: Schedule regular partner meetings to discuss and review the partnership's financial performance, operations, and strategic decisions. These meetings provide a platform for sharing information, addressing concerns, and making collective decisions.

2. Financial Reports and Updates: Prepare and share financial reports on a regular basis to keep all partners informed about the partnership's financial performance. This includes income statements, balance sheets, cash flow statements, and other relevant financial data. Analyze the reports together to identify areas of strength, potential risks, and areas that require attention.

3. Risk Assessment and Mitigation: Engage in ongoing risk assessment and discuss potential risks that may affect the partnership. This includes identifying legal, financial, operational, and market risks. Work collaboratively to develop strategies to mitigate these risks and establish contingency plans.

4. Decision-Making Processes: Establish clear decision-making processes within the partnership. Determine how major decisions will be made, such as financial investments,

expansion plans, or changes in partnership structure. Encourage open discussion and seek consensus whenever possible to ensure that all partners have a voice in the decision-making process.

5. Conflict Resolution: Address conflicts or disagreements that may arise promptly and constructively. Encourage open dialogue and active listening to understand different perspectives. If necessary, engage a neutral third party, such as a mediator or arbitrator, to help facilitate the resolution of conflicts.

6. Document Agreements and Decisions: Keep a record of all agreements and decisions made within the partnership. This includes documenting any changes to the partnership agreement, financial arrangements, or other significant decisions. These records serve as a reference point and help maintain clarity and accountability.

7. Foster a Culture of Trust and Respect: Nurture a culture of trust, respect, and open communication among partners. Encourage an environment where all partners feel comfortable sharing their opinions and ideas. This fosters collaboration and a sense of shared responsibility within the partnership.

8. Seek Professional Advice: When facing complex legal or financial matters, consider seeking professional advice from attorneys, accountants, or business consultants. Their expertise can provide valuable insights and help partners make well-informed decisions.

By maintaining open and transparent communication, partners can effectively manage the partnership's financial affairs, address potential risks, and make informed decisions together. This collaborative approach strengthens the partnership, minimizes liability exposure, and fosters a strong foundation for long-term success.

Professional Guidance: Consulting with an attorney experienced in partnership law is indeed highly recommended for partners in a general partnership. Partnership laws can vary by jurisdiction, and an attorney can provide personalized advice tailored to your specific circumstances.

An experienced attorney can assist partners in drafting or reviewing partnership agreements, which define the rights, responsibilities, and obligations of each partner. They can ensure that the agreement addresses critical aspects such as profit sharing, decision-making processes, dispute resolution mechanisms, and procedures for admitting or withdrawing partners.

Moreover, an attorney can guide partners on risk management strategies to protect personal assets. They can provide insight into potential liability risks and help implement measures to mitigate them. This may include obtaining appropriate insurance coverage, structuring the partnership's activities to minimize risk exposure, and ensuring compliance with legal and regulatory requirements.

In the event of disputes or conflicts among partners, an attorney can facilitate resolution through negotiation, mediation, or, if necessary, litigation. They can protect the interests of individual partners while striving to preserve the integrity and viability of the partnership.

By seeking the advice of an attorney experienced in partnership law, partners can gain a deeper understanding of their rights and obligations, reduce the likelihood of disputes, and protect their personal assets from potential liability. Consulting an attorney ensures that the partnership operates within the boundaries of the law and allows partners to focus on the growth and success of their business.

Limited Partnerships:

Limited partnerships consist of both general partners and limited partners. General partners have unlimited liability and are actively involved in the business's management and decision-making. They assume personal responsibility for the partnership's obligations. Limited partners, on the other hand, have limited liability, meaning their personal assets are generally protected beyond their capital contributions. However, limited partners have restricted control over the partnership's operations and decision-making. They typically invest capital but do not actively participate in day-to-day management.

Partnerships offer several advantages, including flexibility in decision-making and shared responsibilities. Partners can bring different skills, resources, and expertise to the table, which can benefit the business's growth and success. Partnerships also allow for the pooling of financial resources and shared risks.

However, partnerships can face challenges, such as disagreements between partners and the potential for personal liability. Disagreements may arise regarding business decisions, profit sharing, or the direction of the partnership. Clear partnership agreements and communication protocols are essential to mitigate such challenges and foster a harmonious working relationship.

To protect the interests of all partners and establish clear expectations, it is crucial to have a well-drafted partnership agreement that outlines the rights, responsibilities, and decision-making processes. Consulting with an attorney experienced in business law is recommended to ensure that the partnership agreement reflects the partners' intentions and provides adequate protection.

Before entering into a partnership, carefully consider the risks and rewards associated with the structure. Assess your compatibility with potential partners, evaluate the potential liabilities, and establish open lines of communication to address any potential disagreements that may arise.

Limited Liability Company (LLC):

An LLC, or Limited Liability Company, is a business structure that combines the benefits of a corporation and a partnership. It provides limited liability protection to its owners, known as members, while offering flexibility in management and taxation. This hybrid structure has made LLCs a popular choice for small businesses seeking liability protection and tax advantages.

One of the primary advantages of an LLC is the limited liability protection it offers to its members. This means that the personal assets of the members are generally protected from the company's debts and legal obligations. In the event of lawsuits or financial difficulties faced by the LLC, the personal assets of the members are typically not at risk, except in cases of fraud or personal guarantees.

Flexibility in management is another key feature of an LLC. Unlike corporations, LLCs are not bound by strict management structures and formalities. Members have the freedom to structure the company's management as they see fit. They can choose to manage the LLC themselves or appoint managers to handle day-to-day operations. This flexibility allows for efficient decision-making and adaptability in response to changing business needs.

Taxation is another significant benefit of an LLC. By default, an LLC is considered a pass-through entity for tax purposes. This means that the LLC's profits and losses "pass through" to the members' individual tax returns. As a result, the LLC itself does not pay federal income tax, avoiding the issue of double taxation that corporations face. Members report their share of the LLC's profits and losses on their personal tax returns, simplifying the tax process and potentially reducing the overall tax liability.

Furthermore, LLCs offer opportunities for flexible allocation of profits and losses among members. This allows for customized distribution of earnings based on the members' ownership interests or as specified in the operating agreement.

To establish an LLC, it is typically necessary to file the required documents with the state where the business operates, such as Articles of Organization or a Certificate of Formation. It is also advisable to draft an operating agreement that outlines the rights, responsibilities, and operating procedures of the LLC. This agreement helps establish a clear framework for decision-making, profit distribution, and management of the LLC.

Consulting with an attorney or a business advisor experienced in LLC formation is recommended to ensure compliance with state laws and to tailor the LLC structure to your specific business needs. They can provide guidance on the appropriate steps to establish an LLC and assist in drafting the necessary documents.

In summary, an LLC offers a combination of limited liability protection, flexibility in management, and tax advantages. It provides small business owners with personal asset protection while offering the benefits of pass-through taxation and a more adaptable management structure. Consider the advantages and consult with professionals to determine if an LLC is the right choice for your business.

Corporation:

A corporation is indeed a separate legal entity that offers the most extensive liability protection to its shareholders. The liability of shareholders is generally limited to the amount they have invested in the company. This means that personal assets are typically shielded from the corporation's debts and obligations.

One of the significant advantages of a corporation is the ability to raise capital through the sale of shares. Corporations can issue stocks or shares to investors in exchange for capital investment. This makes it easier for corporations to attract funding from external sources, such as venture capitalists, angel investors, or through initial public offerings (IPOs).

Additionally, corporations have perpetual existence. The death, retirement, or transfer of shares by shareholders does not affect the corporation's continuity. This stability is beneficial for long-term business operations and succession planning.

Corporations also provide clear management structures. Shareholders elect a board of directors who are responsible for making strategic decisions and overseeing the corporation's operations. The board appoints officers who handle day-to-day management. This separation of ownership and management can provide clarity and accountability within the corporate structure.

However, it is important to note that corporations require more formalities compared to other business structures. This includes holding regular meetings, maintaining corporate records, and complying with legal and regulatory obligations. Failing to fulfill these formalities can result in loss of liability protection or legal consequences.

Another consideration is the potential for double taxation on corporate profits. Corporations are subject to corporate income tax on their profits. If dividends are distributed to shareholders, those dividends may be subject to individual income tax as well. This can result in the same income being taxed at both the corporate and individual levels. However, certain tax strategies and structures, such as S corporations, can help mitigate the impact of double taxation.

When deciding on a legal structure, it is crucial to consider factors such as personal liability, taxation implications, management structure, and future growth plans. Consulting with an attorney experienced in business law is highly recommended. They can provide valuable guidance tailored to your specific circumstances, help you assess the advantages and disadvantages of each structure, and assist in determining the most suitable option for your business.

Remember, selecting the appropriate legal structure is a critical step in establishing a strong foundation for your business. Seeking professional advice and thoroughly evaluating the implications of each structure are essential for making an informed decision that aligns with your goals and protects your interests.

Understanding business licenses and permits:

Obtaining the necessary licenses and permits is a critical step in ensuring compliance with state and local regulations for your business operations. The specific licenses and permits required can vary based on factors such as your industry, business activities, location, and applicable laws. Thorough research and understanding of the licensing requirements are essential to operate your business legally and avoid potential penalties or disruptions.

To begin, identify the industry-specific licenses and permits that apply to your business. Common examples include professional licenses (e.g., for doctors, lawyers, architects), health and safety permits (e.g., for food service establishments, childcare facilities), environmental permits (e.g., for businesses handling hazardous materials), and specific trade or industry licenses (e.g., for contractors, real estate agents).

Research the specific requirements of the licenses and permits you need. This may include completing application forms, providing documentation, meeting certain qualifications or experience requirements, and paying applicable fees. Engage with the relevant licensing authorities or regulatory agencies at the state, local, or federal level to obtain accurate and up-to-date information on the requirements and application processes.

Complying with licensing requirements often involves demonstrating that your business meets certain standards and regulations. This may include inspections, background checks, proof of insurance coverage, adherence to health and safety protocols, and compliance with zoning and building codes. Be prepared to invest the necessary time, effort, and resources to ensure compliance with all applicable requirements.

Failure to obtain the necessary licenses and permits can result in legal consequences, fines, business closures, or reputational damage. It is therefore essential to prioritize and budget for these requirements as part of your business planning process.

Seeking professional guidance from attorneys specializing in business law or consultants experienced in regulatory compliance can provide valuable assistance throughout the licensing process. They can help you understand the specific requirements, assist with completing applications, review documentation, and ensure that you meet all obligations for obtaining and maintaining the necessary licenses and permits.

Remember that licensing requirements may evolve over time due to changes in laws or regulations. Regularly review your licensing obligations to ensure ongoing compliance and stay updated on any changes that may affect your business. By obtaining the necessary licenses and permits, you demonstrate your commitment to legal and ethical business practices, protect the well-being of your customers and employees, and contribute to the long-term success and sustainability of your business.

Zoning Permits:

Zoning permits play a crucial role in ensuring that your business operates in compliance with local zoning regulations. Zoning regulations are established by local governments to control land use and designate specific areas for different types of activities, such as residential, commercial, industrial, or mixed-use.

Zoning permits confirm that your business activities align with the designated zoning for the area where your business is located. These permits help maintain a cohesive community by ensuring that businesses are appropriately situated, taking into account factors such as traffic flow, noise levels, environmental impact, and community aesthetics.

Zoning laws can vary widely from one jurisdiction to another, and even within different zones within the same jurisdiction. These regulations may dictate the types of businesses allowed in specific zones, such as retail, restaurants, professional services, or industrial operations. They may also establish restrictions on building height, signage, parking, and other considerations.

To obtain a zoning permit, you will typically need to submit an application to the local zoning or planning department. The application may require information about your business activities, the type of property you intend to use, and how it aligns with the designated zoning. The zoning authorities will review your application to ensure compliance with the applicable zoning regulations.

It is important to note that zoning regulations may be subject to change, and new zoning restrictions or updates may be implemented over time. Therefore, it is crucial to consult with local zoning authorities or engage with professionals who specialize in zoning and land use regulations to ensure that you have the most up-to-date information.

Non-compliance with zoning regulations can result in legal consequences, fines, or even the forced closure of your business. Therefore, it is essential to understand and adhere to the zoning requirements specific to your business location.

Working with attorneys specializing in zoning and land use law or consultants experienced in navigating zoning regulations can provide valuable guidance and assistance. They can help you understand the specific zoning requirements applicable to your business, assist with the application process, and ensure that your business operations comply with all relevant zoning regulations.

By obtaining the necessary zoning permits and adhering to zoning regulations, you demonstrate your commitment to operating your business in a manner that respects the interests of the community and contributes to a well-organized and harmonious environment.

Health and Safety Permits:

Health and safety permits are crucial for businesses operating in industries where the well-being of employees and the public is of paramount importance. These permits ensure that your business meets specific health and safety standards established by regulatory authorities. They are particularly relevant in industries such as food service, healthcare, child care, or manufacturing, where potential risks and hazards exist.

Obtaining health and safety permits demonstrates your commitment to maintaining a safe and healthy environment for employees, customers, and the community at large. By complying with these requirements, you reduce the risk of accidents, injuries, and the spread of diseases, ensuring the well-being of all stakeholders involved.

Examples of health and safety permits include:

Food Handling Permits:

If your business involves food service, it is essential to comply with the applicable regulations and obtain the necessary permits to ensure food safety. In Florida, food handling permits or food service establishment licenses may be required depending on the nature of your food-related activities.

Food handling permits and food service establishment licenses are typically issued by the Florida Department of Business and Professional

Regulation (DBPR) or the local health department. These permits and licenses ensure that your business meets specific hygiene standards, safe food handling practices, and health regulations.

To obtain a food handling permit or food service establishment license, you will likely need to demonstrate compliance with various requirements, such as:

1. Safe Food Handling Practices: Your business must adhere to proper food handling, storage, preparation, and cooking practices to prevent contamination and ensure food safety.
2. Sanitation and Hygiene: Maintain a clean and sanitary environment in your food service establishment. This includes regular cleaning and sanitization of equipment, utensils, surfaces, and facilities.
3. Employee Training: Ensure that employees involved in food handling receive appropriate training in safe food practices, personal hygiene, and sanitation.
4. Food Safety Plans: Develop and implement a food safety plan that outlines procedures for handling, storing, and serving food, as well as protocols for responding to food-related emergencies.
5. Inspections: Expect periodic inspections by health department officials to evaluate your compliance with food safety regulations. Cooperate with inspectors and address any issues or deficiencies promptly.

It is important to note that specific requirements and regulations can vary depending on the location and type of food service establishment. Therefore, it is advisable to consult with the Florida Department of Business and Professional Regulation or the local health department to understand the specific requirements for your business.

By obtaining the necessary permits and adhering to food safety regulations, you can demonstrate your commitment to providing safe and hygienic food to your customers. This not only protects the health and well-being of consumers but also helps build trust and credibility for your food service business.

Fire Safety Inspections:

Fire safety permits and inspections are indeed crucial for ensuring the safety of your business premises and compliance with fire safety regulations. These permits and inspections are typically conducted by the local fire department or fire marshal's office in accordance with state and local laws.

The purpose of fire safety permits and inspections is to assess and verify that your business premises meet the necessary fire safety standards and have appropriate measures in place to prevent fires and protect occupants in case of emergencies. Here are some key aspects related to fire safety permits and inspections:

1. Fire Suppression Systems: Fire safety inspections may include an evaluation of fire suppression systems, such as fire sprinklers, fire extinguishers, and fire alarms. These systems should be properly installed, maintained, and functional to effectively detect and suppress fires.
2. Emergency Exits and Egress Routes: Inspectors will assess the availability, condition, and proper signage of emergency exits and egress routes. These exits and routes should be unobstructed, well-marked, and easily accessible to ensure safe evacuation in case of a fire or other emergencies.
3. Electrical and Wiring Systems: Fire safety inspections may include a review of electrical systems, wiring, and other potential fire hazards. Ensuring that electrical systems are up to code and properly maintained can help prevent electrical fires.
4. Hazardous Materials and Storage: If your business involves the use or storage of hazardous materials, inspectors will assess compliance with regulations regarding their safe handling, storage, and disposal to minimize the risk of fire incidents.
5. Emergency Response and Fire Safety Plans: Inspectors may review your business's emergency response plans, including fire evacuation plans, employee training, and communication protocols. Having well-developed plans and training in place demonstrates your commitment to fire safety.

Non-compliance with fire safety regulations can result in penalties, fines, or even closure of your business. It is crucial to stay informed about the specific fire safety requirements applicable to your business location and industry. Regularly review and maintain fire safety measures, conduct fire drills, and address any identified deficiencies promptly to ensure the safety of your employees, customers, and property.

Consulting with fire safety professionals or contacting your local fire department can provide guidance on specific requirements and help ensure that your business is adequately protected against fire hazards. By prioritizing fire safety and obtaining the necessary permits and inspections, you demonstrate your commitment to the well-being of your employees and the community.

Occupational Safety Certifications:

Certain industries, such as construction or manufacturing, may require occupational safety certifications. These certifications ensure that your business complies with safety regulations regarding machinery usage, personal protective equipment, hazardous materials handling, and other workplace safety measures.

Other health and safety permits may be specific to the industry or the nature of your business. Examples include permits for handling hazardous materials, operating medical facilities, providing child care services, or maintaining swimming pools or spas. These permits typically involve inspections, compliance with specific regulations, and ongoing monitoring to ensure continued adherence to health and safety standards.

It is crucial to research and understand the specific health and safety permits required for your industry and business operations. Consult with local health departments, regulatory agencies, or industry associations to obtain accurate information regarding the permits applicable to your business.

Working with health and safety professionals, such as occupational health and safety consultants or environmental health officers, can provide valuable guidance in navigating the complex regulatory landscape. They can help you assess your business's specific health and safety needs, ensure compliance with regulations, and guide you through the permit application and inspection processes.

By obtaining the necessary health and safety permits and adhering to the prescribed standards, you demonstrate your commitment to the well-being of employees, customers, and the community. Prioritizing health and safety not only protects individuals but also enhances the reputation and credibility of your business.

Professional Licensing:

Professional licenses are essential for certain occupations and professions to ensure competence and protect the public interest. These licenses are typically required for professions that have a direct impact on the health, safety, or well-being of individuals or involve specialized expertise. Examples of professions that commonly require professional licenses include doctors, lawyers, accountants, architects, and real estate agents.

Obtaining a professional license involves meeting specific requirements established by regulatory bodies or professional organizations. These requirements often include a combination of education, examinations, practical experience, and adherence to ethical standards.

1. Education: Professional licenses often require completion of specific educational programs from accredited institutions. These programs ensure that individuals have the necessary knowledge and skills to practice their profession competently. The duration and nature of the required education can vary depending on the profession and jurisdiction.

2. Examinations: Professionals seeking licenses may need to pass rigorous examinations to demonstrate their proficiency in their respective fields. These examinations assess the knowledge, critical thinking abilities, and application of principles relevant to the profession.

3. Practical Experience: In some cases, professional licenses may require a certain amount of practical experience or apprenticeship under the supervision of experienced professionals. This requirement ensures that individuals have practical skills and real-world experience before entering independent practice.

4. Continuing Education: Many professional licenses also have ongoing requirements for continuing education or professional development. These requirements ensure that professionals stay updated on the latest developments, best practices, and ethical standards in their field. Continuing education helps maintain competence and ensures that professionals provide high-quality services to the public.

Obtaining and maintaining a professional license demonstrates a commitment to professional standards, ethical conduct, and ongoing learning. It provides assurance to clients, employers, and the public that professionals have met specific competency requirements and are held accountable for their actions.

It is important to note that the requirements for professional licenses can vary across jurisdictions. It is essential to consult the relevant regulatory bodies or professional organizations in your jurisdiction to understand the specific requirements for your profession.

Failure to obtain the necessary professional license can result in legal consequences, including fines, penalties, or restrictions on practicing the profession. Engaging with professional associations, attending informational sessions, and seeking guidance from experienced professionals in your field can provide valuable insights and support throughout the licensing process.

By obtaining and maintaining a professional license, professionals demonstrate their dedication to their field and their commitment to providing quality services while upholding professional standards and ethics.

Business Registration and Taxation:

Registering your business with the appropriate state and local agencies is an essential step in establishing your business's legal presence and ensuring compliance with regulatory requirements. This process involves several key registrations and obligations that vary by state. Here are some important considerations:

State Tax Identification Number:

Registering for a state tax identification number, also known as an Employer Identification Number (EIN) or a State Tax ID, is indeed a necessary step for many businesses. This unique identifier is assigned by the state tax authority and is used to identify your business for various tax-related purposes.

Here are some key points to consider regarding state tax identification numbers:

1. Requirement for Hiring Employees: If your business plans to hire employees, an EIN is generally required. This identification number is used to report employment taxes, such as federal and state income tax withholding, Social Security, and Medicare taxes.
2. Tax Return Filings: An EIN is typically needed when filing tax returns for your business entity. It ensures that your business is properly identified by the tax authorities and helps facilitate the processing of your tax filings.
3. Opening Bank Accounts: Financial institutions often require an EIN to open a business bank account. This number establishes

your business's tax identification and assists in separating personal and business finances.

4. Business Transactions: In certain situations, such as applying for business credit or entering into financial transactions, having an EIN may be necessary for proper identification and record-keeping purposes.

The process of obtaining an EIN varies depending on the state in which your business operates. In many cases, you can apply for an EIN online through the state tax authority's website or by completing a paper application and submitting it by mail. The application typically requires basic information about your business, such as its legal name, address, and nature of operations.

It is important to note that an EIN is different from a federal Employer Identification Number issued by the Internal Revenue Service (IRS). While some states may use the same identification number for both state and federal tax purposes, others have separate state identification numbers.

To determine the specific requirements and procedures for obtaining a state tax identification number in Florida, it is recommended to visit the website of the Florida Department of Revenue or consult with a qualified tax professional.

By registering for a state tax identification number, you ensure that your business is properly identified for tax purposes and can fulfill its tax obligations. This identification number plays a critical role in various business transactions and helps maintain compliance with state tax regulations.

Sales Tax Registration:

If your business sells tangible goods or certain services, it is indeed important to register for sales tax with your state's revenue or taxation department. Sales tax registration allows your business to collect sales tax from customers and remit it to the appropriate state authorities.

Here are key points to consider regarding sales tax registration:

1. Determine Sales Tax Nexus: Sales tax nexus refers to the connection between your business and a state that requires you to collect and remit sales tax. Nexus can be established through various factors, such as having a physical presence (e.g., a physical location, employees, or inventory) or reaching

certain sales thresholds in a particular state. It is crucial to understand the nexus requirements in each state where you have a sales presence.

2. Register with the State Revenue Department: Once you have determined your sales tax nexus, you will need to register with the revenue or taxation department of each state where you have nexus. The registration process typically involves completing an application, providing relevant business information, and obtaining a sales tax permit or certificate.

3. Collecting Sales Tax: After registration, you are responsible for collecting sales tax from customers on taxable transactions. The sales tax rate and taxable items can vary by state and sometimes by locality within the state. Ensure that you are charging the correct sales tax rate based on the customer's location and the specific products or services sold.

4. Filing Sales Tax Returns: Depending on the state, you will need to file sales tax returns periodically, typically monthly, quarterly, or annually. These returns report the sales tax you have collected and remitted during the reporting period. It is crucial to accurately calculate and report your sales tax liability to remain compliant with state regulations.

5. Record-Keeping: Maintaining detailed records of your sales transactions, including invoices, receipts, and sales tax collected, is essential for sales tax compliance. These records should be kept for a specified period as required by state regulations.

6. Stay Updated on Sales Tax Changes: Sales tax regulations can change over time, so it is important to stay informed about any updates or modifications to the sales tax laws in the states where you operate. This may include changes in tax rates, exemptions, filing requirements, or reporting obligations.

To ensure compliance with sales tax regulations, consider consulting with a tax professional or accountant who is knowledgeable about sales tax laws in your state. They can provide guidance on registration requirements, sales tax collection, and filing obligations specific to your business.

Remember, sales tax registration and compliance are crucial for avoiding penalties, maintaining good standing with state authorities, and operating your business legally. By understanding and adhering to the sales tax regulations in your state, you can fulfill your tax obligations and minimize the risk of costly non-compliance issues.

Business Entity Registration:

Registering your business entity is indeed a crucial step in establishing its legal existence and ensuring compliance with state regulations. The registration process involves filing the necessary formation documents with the appropriate state agency, such as the Secretary of State or the Corporations Division.

Here are some key points to consider when registering your business entity:

1. Choose a Business Structure: Before registering, determine the most suitable business structure for your needs. Common options include sole proprietorship, partnership, limited liability company (LLC), and corporation. Each structure has different legal and tax implications, so it is important to understand the advantages and disadvantages of each.
2. Select a Business Name: Choose a unique and distinguishable name for your business. Conduct a thorough search to ensure that the name you want is available and not already in use by another entity. Some states may have specific naming requirements or restrictions, so it is important to check the guidelines set by the state agency where you are registering.
3. Prepare Formation Documents: Depending on your chosen business structure, you will need to prepare the appropriate formation documents. These may include articles of organization for an LLC, a certificate of partnership for a partnership, or articles of incorporation for a corporation. The specific information and details required in these documents may vary by state.
4. File Registration Documents: Once you have prepared the necessary formation documents, file them with the appropriate state agency. This typically involves submitting the documents along with the required filing fees. Some states may also require additional forms or disclosures, such as an operating agreement for an LLC or bylaws for a corporation.
5. Obtain Necessary Permits and Licenses: Depending on the nature of your business and its location, you may need to obtain additional permits or licenses from state or local

authorities. Research the specific requirements for your industry to ensure compliance and avoid potential legal issues.

6. Maintain Compliance: After registering your business entity, it is important to maintain compliance with ongoing filing and reporting requirements. This may include filing annual reports, updating registration information, and renewing licenses or permits as necessary. Failure to comply with these requirements can result in penalties or the loss of your business's legal status.

Consulting with an attorney or business advisor who specializes in business formation and registration can provide valuable guidance throughout the process. They can help you understand the specific requirements in your state, ensure that you complete the necessary documentation accurately, and assist with any additional compliance obligations.

Remember, registering your business entity establishes its legal existence and provides you with certain rights and protections. By following the proper registration procedures and maintaining compliance with state regulations, you can lay a solid foundation for your business and mitigate potential legal risks.

Doing Business As (DBA) Registration:

If you choose to operate your business under a name different from your legal entity's name, registering a "Doing Business As" (DBA) or "Fictitious Name" is indeed an important step. This registration allows you to conduct business under your chosen name while ensuring transparency and compliance with state regulations.

Here are some key points to consider when registering a DBA or Fictitious Name:

1. Determine the Need for a DBA: If you plan to operate your business using a name other than your legal entity's name (such as using a trade name or a brand name), you will likely need to register a DBA. This is especially relevant for sole proprietorships, partnerships, or LLCs that want to operate under a different name.

2. Conduct a Name Search: Before registering a DBA, conduct a thorough search to ensure that the name you want is available and not already in use by another business. This helps avoid potential conflicts or confusion in the marketplace. Many states

have online databases or resources where you can check the availability of a DBA.

3. Understand State Requirements: Familiarize yourself with the specific requirements for registering a DBA in your state. Some states may require you to file the registration with the Secretary of State, while others may require you to file with the county clerk's office or another designated agency. Additionally, some states may have specific forms or fees associated with the registration.

4. Prepare and File the Registration: Once you have completed the necessary research and obtained the required forms, prepare the registration documents. This typically includes providing information such as your legal entity's name, the desired DBA name, and your contact information. Submit the completed registration form along with any required fees to the appropriate agency.

5. Publish or Renew, if Required: In some states, after registering a DBA, you may be required to publish a notice in a local newspaper to inform the public of your new business name. Additionally, be aware of any renewal requirements for your DBA registration. Some states may require periodic renewals to ensure the accuracy of the registration.

6. Update Business Records: Once your DBA is registered, update your business records and licenses accordingly. This includes updating your bank accounts, obtaining new licenses or permits under the DBA name, and updating your marketing materials and online presence to reflect the new name.

It is important to consult with an attorney or business advisor who is familiar with the registration process in your specific state. They can guide you through the necessary steps, ensure compliance with state regulations, and address any questions or concerns you may have.

By registering a DBA, you can legally conduct business under your chosen name while maintaining transparency and compliance with state regulations. This allows you to operate under a name that reflects your brand and effectively represents your business in the marketplace.

Professional Licensing:

Certain professions indeed require professional licensing in addition to business registration. Professions such as doctors, lawyers, engineers, architects, real estate agents, and many others are subject to licensing requirements imposed by specialized regulatory agencies or professional boards. These requirements aim to ensure that practitioners have the necessary qualifications, knowledge, and skills to provide services in their respective fields.

The process of obtaining a professional license typically involves the following steps:

1. Education and Training: Most professions require completion of specific educational programs from accredited institutions. This may include earning a bachelor's degree, completing a professional degree program, or fulfilling specialized training requirements.
2. Examination: After completing the required education or training, aspiring professionals often need to pass a licensing examination. These examinations assess their knowledge and competence in the field and may be administered by state licensing boards or national organizations.
3. Experience: Some professions require a certain amount of practical experience before obtaining a license. This may involve completing an internship, residency, or supervised work under a licensed professional.
4. Application and Documentation: Once the educational, examination, and experience requirements are met, individuals can submit an application for licensure to the relevant licensing authority. This typically involves completing an application form, providing supporting documents such as transcripts, examination results, and letters of recommendation, and paying the required fees.
5. Background Check: In many cases, a background check is conducted as part of the licensing process. This ensures that applicants have a good professional standing and do not have a history of disciplinary actions or criminal offenses that would impede their ability to practice in the profession.
6. Ongoing Continuing Education: After obtaining a professional license, practitioners are often required to engage in continuing education activities to maintain their knowledge and skills. This ensures that professionals stay up-to-date with the latest developments in their field and continue to provide high-quality services.

It is important to note that licensing requirements vary by profession and by state. Therefore, it is essential for individuals pursuing a licensed profession to research and understand the specific requirements in their jurisdiction. Consulting with the appropriate licensing board or regulatory agency can provide the most accurate and up-to-date information regarding the licensure process.

By obtaining a professional license, individuals demonstrate their qualifications and commitment to practicing their profession at a high standard. This not only ensures public safety but also instills confidence in clients and establishes professional credibility within the industry.

Employer Registration:

If you plan to hire employees, it is indeed important to register with the appropriate state agency responsible for unemployment insurance and workers' compensation. This registration ensures compliance with labor laws and enables you to fulfill your obligations as an employer.

The specific registration requirements and obligations related to hiring employees may vary by state. It is crucial to thoroughly research and understand the requirements in the state where you plan to operate. This includes identifying the agency responsible for managing unemployment insurance and workers' compensation and familiarizing yourself with their processes and procedures.

Registering for unemployment insurance typically involves providing information about your business, such as its legal name, business address, federal employer identification number (FEIN), and the names and Social Security numbers of your employees. This information helps establish your business's account with the state unemployment insurance program, enabling you to report wages and pay the required unemployment insurance taxes.

Workers' compensation registration involves obtaining the necessary insurance coverage to protect your employees in case of work-related injuries or illnesses. This coverage provides medical benefits and wage replacement for injured employees and helps protect your business from potential liability. Requirements for workers' compensation insurance vary by state, and it is essential to consult with an insurance professional or an attorney specializing in workers' compensation to ensure compliance with the specific regulations in your state.

Failure to register for unemployment insurance and workers' compensation or comply with related obligations can result in penalties and legal consequences. It is important to prioritize these registrations and fulfill your obligations as an employer to maintain compliance with labor laws and provide a safe and fair working environment for your employees.

To navigate the registration process and understand your obligations, consider utilizing resources such as state government websites, local business development centers, or professional advisors specializing in business law or human resources. These resources can provide valuable guidance tailored to your specific circumstances and help ensure that you meet the necessary requirements to operate your business legally and responsibly.

By fulfilling the necessary registrations and complying with your obligations as an employer, you establish a solid foundation for your business operations, protect your employees, and demonstrate your commitment to operating your business in accordance with applicable labor laws and regulations.

Industry-Specific Permits:

Certain industries have unique licensing requirements. For example, contractors may need contractor licenses, transportation businesses may need permits for commercial vehicles, and liquor establishments may need liquor licenses. Researching industry-specific regulations and obtaining the necessary permits ensures compliance and enables lawful operation.

To navigate the licensing process effectively, it is recommended to consult with professionals familiar with licensing and permitting requirements in your industry and location. Attorneys specializing in business law or consultants experienced in regulatory compliance can provide guidance tailored to your specific needs. They can assist in researching the requirements, preparing the necessary documentation, and submitting applications to obtain the required licenses and permits.

By investing time and effort into understanding and fulfilling licensing and permitting requirements, you ensure that your business operates legally, mitigates risks, and demonstrates a commitment to compliance and the well-being of your employees and the public.

Conducting market research:

Thorough market research is an indispensable aspect of establishing and operating a successful business. It provides you with a deep understanding of your target market, competitors, and industry trends. This knowledge allows you to make informed decisions, develop effective strategies, and create a unique value proposition that resonates with your customers.

One of the primary benefits of market research is gaining insights into your target audience. By understanding the needs, preferences, and behaviors of your potential customers, you can tailor your products or services to meet their specific demands. Market research helps you identify your target market segments, their demographics, psychographics, and purchasing patterns. This information enables you to develop effective marketing strategies, positioning your business to reach the right customers with the right messages.

Additionally, market research helps you assess the competitive landscape. By analyzing your competitors' strengths, weaknesses, and market positioning, you can identify opportunities for differentiation and innovation. Understanding how your competitors operate and how they meet customer needs allows you to develop strategies that set your business apart and give you a competitive advantage.

Market research also helps you stay updated on industry trends and market dynamics. By tracking market trends, technological advancements, and consumer behavior shifts, you can proactively adapt your business strategies to stay ahead of the curve. This knowledge allows you to identify emerging opportunities, anticipate challenges, and make data-driven decisions that drive growth and profitability.

There are various methods and techniques for conducting market research, including surveys, interviews, focus groups, data analysis, and competitor analysis. It is essential to use a combination of primary and secondary research methods to gather comprehensive and reliable data. Primary research involves collecting data directly from your target audience, while secondary research involves analyzing existing sources such as industry reports, government data, and market studies.

Engaging with professional market research firms, utilizing online research tools, and seeking feedback from potential customers can enhance the effectiveness of your research efforts. These resources can provide valuable insights and help validate your assumptions, ensuring that your business strategies are based on reliable data.

In conclusion, thorough market research is a critical component of establishing a successful business. It allows you to identify market opportunities, understand customer needs, differentiate from competitors, and adapt to evolving market trends. By investing time and effort in market research, you position your business for long-term success and growth.

Understanding Your Target Audience:

Market research plays a crucial role in gaining a deep understanding of your target audience. By conducting thorough analysis of demographics, psychographics, and consumer behavior, you can uncover valuable insights that inform your business strategies and marketing efforts.

Demographic information encompasses characteristics such as age, gender, income, education, and geographic location. Understanding these factors helps you identify the specific groups of individuals or businesses that are most likely to have an interest in your products or services. Demographic data provides a foundation for segmenting your target audience and customizing your marketing messages to reach and resonate with each segment effectively.

Psychographic information delves into the psychological and behavioral aspects of your target audience. It includes factors such as values, attitudes, interests, lifestyle choices, and motivations. Psychographics help you gain insights into what drives your audience's purchasing decisions and how they perceive and interact with your products or services. This knowledge enables you to tailor your offerings and marketing messages to align with their preferences and desires.

Consumer behavior analysis involves studying how your target audience behaves in relation to your products or services. This includes their purchasing habits, decision-making processes, brand loyalty, and response to marketing stimuli. By understanding consumer behavior, you can identify the key factors that influence their purchasing decisions and craft marketing strategies that effectively appeal to their needs and preferences.

With a comprehensive understanding of your target audience, you can tailor your products, services, and marketing messages to address their specific needs, pain points, and desires. By developing targeted marketing campaigns, personalized messaging, and tailored offers, you can effectively engage and resonate with your target audience, increasing the likelihood of conversion and building long-term customer relationships.

Market research methods such as surveys, interviews, focus groups, and data analysis can help you gather the necessary information about your target audience. Additionally, leveraging data from market research firms, industry reports, and customer feedback can enhance your understanding of your target audience's needs and preferences.

By investing time and resources into market research, you position your business to make informed decisions, create customer-centric strategies, and deliver products or services that meet the specific demands of your target audience. This understanding is instrumental in building strong brand loyalty, driving customer satisfaction, and achieving business success.

Assessing the Competitive Landscape:

Market research plays a vital role in analyzing and assessing your competitors, allowing you to gain valuable insights into their strategies, products, and positioning. By studying your competitors, you can identify opportunities for differentiation, assess market trends, and develop effective strategies to gain a competitive edge. Here's how market research helps you in analyzing your competitors:

1. Product Analysis: Through market research, you can examine your competitors' products or services. This includes understanding their features, quality, pricing, and unique selling points. By comparing your offerings to those of your competitors, you can identify areas where you can differentiate or enhance your own products to meet customer needs more effectively.
2. Pricing Strategies: Market research enables you to evaluate the pricing strategies of your competitors. By understanding their pricing models, discounts, promotions, and value propositions, you can assess whether your prices are competitive in the market. This analysis can help you determine if there is room for adjustments to attract customers or position your products or services as premium offerings.

3. Marketing Tactics: Studying your competitors' marketing tactics provides insights into their promotional activities, advertising campaigns, and customer engagement strategies. By analyzing their messaging, channels, and target audience, you can identify gaps or opportunities to differentiate your own marketing efforts. This understanding helps you craft effective marketing strategies that resonate with your target market and stand out from the competition.

4. Customer Reviews and Feedback: Market research allows you to gather and analyze customer reviews and feedback about your competitors' products or services. By understanding what customers appreciate or dislike about your competitors, you can identify areas where you can outperform or address gaps in the market. This knowledge helps you tailor your offerings to meet customer expectations and improve customer satisfaction.

5. Strengths and Weaknesses: Through market research, you can identify your competitors' strengths and weaknesses. By evaluating their market share, customer loyalty, reputation, and operational capabilities, you gain insights into their competitive advantages and areas where they may be vulnerable. This analysis enables you to capitalize on your strengths and develop strategies to exploit your competitors' weaknesses.

By conducting comprehensive market research on your competitors, you can develop a deep understanding of their strategies, products, and customer perception. This knowledge allows you to position your business uniquely and develop effective strategies to gain a competitive edge. It empowers you to differentiate your offerings, enhance your value proposition, and capture a larger share of the market. Ultimately, market research serves as a critical tool in shaping your competitive strategy and achieving long-term success in your industry.

Identifying Market Trends:

Market research is an invaluable tool for staying informed about the latest trends and shifts in the market. It enables you to monitor industry reports, consumer surveys, and social media discussions, providing you with insights into emerging trends, changing consumer preferences, and technological advancements. Here's how market research helps you stay ahead of the competition:

1. Identify Emerging Trends: By analyzing market research data, you can identify emerging trends that may impact your industry. This includes shifts in consumer behavior, technological advancements, changing regulations, or market disruptions. Staying ahead of emerging trends allows you to adapt your business strategies proactively and seize new opportunities before your competitors.
2. Understand Consumer Preferences: Market research helps you gauge consumer preferences and expectations. By analyzing consumer surveys, focus groups, and social media discussions, you can gain insights into what drives consumer purchasing decisions, their preferences for products or services, and their evolving needs. This understanding enables you to tailor your offerings to meet consumer demands and stay relevant in the market.
3. Monitor Competitor Strategies: Through market research, you can keep track of your competitors' strategies and activities. This includes monitoring their product launches, pricing changes, marketing campaigns, and customer feedback. By staying informed about your competitors, you can identify areas where you can differentiate or improve your own strategies to maintain a competitive edge.
4. Spot Technological Advancements: Market research helps you stay updated on technological advancements relevant to your industry. By monitoring industry reports, attending conferences, and engaging with experts, you can identify new technologies, innovative solutions, or process improvements that can enhance your business operations or create new business opportunities. Embracing technological advancements gives you a competitive advantage and allows you to meet evolving customer expectations.
5. Anticipate Market Shifts: Market research helps you anticipate market shifts and adapt accordingly. By analyzing market trends, economic indicators, and consumer behavior patterns, you can identify potential shifts in demand, market saturation, or emerging market segments. This foresight enables you to adjust your business strategies, target new customer segments, or diversify your offerings to stay ahead of market changes.

Regularly conducting market research and staying up-to-date with industry developments positions your business to adapt quickly, innovate, and respond effectively to changing market dynamics. By proactively identifying trends, understanding consumer preferences, monitoring competitors, and embracing technological advancements, you can stay ahead of the competition, maintain relevance, and drive long-term business success.

Remember, market research is an ongoing process that requires continuous monitoring and analysis to ensure you have the most up-to-date information. Investing in market research empowers you to make informed decisions, identify growth opportunities, and navigate market challenges with confidence.

Assessing Market Demand and Opportunities:

Market research is an invaluable tool for assessing the demand for your products or services. It enables you to analyze various factors such as market size, growth rates, and customer needs, helping you identify gaps or underserved segments. This understanding allows you to uncover potential opportunities and shape your business offerings to meet the unmet needs of the market.

1. Market Size: Market research helps you gauge the size of the market you plan to enter. By analyzing industry reports, market data, and demographic information, you can estimate the potential customer base and the overall demand for your products or services. Understanding the market size provides valuable insights into the growth potential and revenue opportunities for your business.
2. Growth Rates: Evaluating market growth rates allows you to identify industries or segments that are experiencing rapid expansion. By examining historical data and projections, you can assess the future demand for your offerings. Targeting growing markets positions your business to capture a larger share and capitalize on emerging opportunities.
3. Customer Needs and Preferences: Market research helps you understand the needs, preferences, and pain points of your target customers. Through surveys, focus groups, and customer feedback, you can gain insights into what customers value, what challenges they face, and what solutions they seek. This knowledge enables you to develop products or services that address those needs and provide value to your target audience.
4. Identify Gaps and Underserved Segments: Through market research, you can identify gaps or underserved segments within

the market. By analyzing competitors, consumer trends, and customer feedback, you can identify areas where existing products or services are not fully meeting customer needs or where there is a lack of offerings altogether. These gaps present opportunities for you to position your business and tailor your offerings to fill those voids.

5. Competitive Analysis: Market research helps you understand the competitive landscape and how your offerings compare to those of your competitors. By analyzing competitor strengths and weaknesses, pricing strategies, and value propositions, you can identify areas where you can differentiate and offer unique value to customers. This analysis allows you to position your business as a preferred choice and attract customers who are looking for alternatives.

By leveraging market research insights, you can shape your business offerings, develop targeted marketing strategies, and optimize your value proposition to align with the demands of the market. It empowers you to meet customer needs effectively, outperform competitors, and capture a larger market share.

Remember, market research is an ongoing process, and regularly monitoring and analyzing market trends and customer feedback is essential to stay responsive to changing demands. By incorporating market research into your business strategy, you can make informed decisions, enhance your competitive advantage, and drive the success and growth of your business.

Refining Business Strategies:

Market research plays a crucial role in refining your business strategies by providing data-driven insights that inform decision-making across various aspects of your business. Here's how market research can help you refine your strategies:

1. Pricing Strategies: Market research enables you to understand customer perceptions of value, competitive pricing, and pricing elasticity. By analyzing pricing data and customer feedback, you can determine the optimal price points for your products or services. This insight helps you set competitive prices that align with customer expectations and maximize profitability.

2. Product Development: Through market research, you can gather feedback on existing products or services and identify

areas for improvement or innovation. By understanding customer needs, preferences, and pain points, you can refine your product offerings to better meet their expectations. This insight guides product development efforts, ensuring that you deliver solutions that resonate with your target audience.

3. Distribution Channels: Market research helps you evaluate different distribution channels and assess their effectiveness in reaching your target market. By analyzing customer behavior and preferences, you can determine the most suitable channels for distributing your products or services. This insight allows you to optimize your distribution strategies, ensuring that your offerings are accessible and available to your target audience.

4. Marketing Campaigns: By conducting market research, you gain insights into customer demographics, psychographics, and preferences. This information enables you to tailor your marketing messages, channels, and tactics to effectively reach and engage your target audience. Market research also helps you identify the most suitable platforms and influencers for promoting your offerings, maximizing the impact of your marketing campaigns.

5. Market Entry Strategies: If you are planning to enter a new market or expand into a new geographic area, market research provides essential insights. It helps you understand the local market dynamics, consumer behavior, competition, and regulatory environment. This knowledge allows you to tailor your market entry strategies and minimize risks associated with entering new markets.

6. Risk Mitigation: Market research helps you assess the potential risks and challenges associated with your business strategies. By identifying market trends, customer preferences, and competitive forces, you can anticipate potential obstacles and develop contingency plans. This proactive approach allows you to mitigate risks and make informed decisions that reduce the likelihood of failure or setbacks.

By aligning your business strategies with the insights gained from market research, you increase the likelihood of success and minimize the risks associated with launching new products or entering new markets. Market research empowers you to make data-driven decisions, optimize your strategies, and adapt to the ever-changing market landscape. It ensures that your business is responsive to customer needs, competitive forces, and market realities, positioning you for long-term growth and profitability.

Developing a Unique Value Proposition:

Market research plays a critical role in developing a unique value proposition for your business. It provides the necessary insights to understand your target audience, competition, and market trends, which are essential in shaping your value proposition. Here's how market research helps in this process:

1. Understanding Your Target Audience: Market research enables you to gain a deep understanding of your target audience's needs, preferences, and pain points. By analyzing demographic, psychographic, and behavioral data, you can identify what matters most to your customers and tailor your value proposition to address their specific needs. This understanding helps you position your products or services as the solution that uniquely meets their requirements.

2. Analyzing Competitor Offerings: Through market research, you can assess your competitors' products or services, pricing, and marketing strategies. By understanding what your competitors are offering and how they position themselves, you can identify gaps or areas where you can differentiate. This insight allows you to craft a value proposition that sets your business apart from the competition and offers unique benefits to your target audience.

3. Identifying Market Trends: Market research helps you stay informed about the latest market trends and shifts in consumer behavior. By monitoring industry reports, consumer surveys, and social media discussions, you can identify emerging needs, changing preferences, and evolving market demands. This knowledge enables you to align your value proposition with current trends and position your business as innovative and responsive to market dynamics.

4. Highlighting Unique Features and Benefits: Through market research, you can identify the unique features, benefits, or qualities of your products or services that differentiate you from competitors. By understanding what aspects of your offerings resonate most with customers, you can emphasize these unique selling points in your value proposition. This helps

communicate the value customers can expect from choosing your business over others.

5. Communicating Effectively: Market research provides insights into the language, messaging, and channels that resonate with your target audience. By understanding their communication preferences, pain points, and aspirations, you can craft compelling and relevant messages that effectively communicate your value proposition. This ensures that your marketing efforts effectively engage and attract your target audience.

Developing a unique value proposition requires a deep understanding of your target audience, competition, and market trends. By leveraging market research insights, you can create a value proposition that clearly communicates the unique benefits your business offers, addresses customer needs, and differentiates you from competitors. A strong value proposition sets the foundation for building brand loyalty, attracting customers, and achieving sustainable business growth.

By conducting thorough market research, you gain a competitive advantage and increase the chances of success for your business. Whether through surveys, focus groups, competitor analysis, or trend monitoring, investing in market research provides valuable insights that inform your decision-making process. Consider engaging market research professionals or utilizing online research tools to ensure the accuracy and reliability of your findings.

Remember, market research is an ongoing process. Regularly monitor changes in your target audience, competition, and industry to stay ahead of the curve and adapt your strategies accordingly. By leveraging market research, you position your business for growth, profitability, and long-term success.

Developing a business plan:

A well-crafted business plan is a fundamental document that guides the trajectory of your business. It serves as a roadmap, outlining your goals, strategies, and financial projections, and providing a comprehensive overview of your business. Whether you are seeking funding, partnerships, or aligning your team around a common vision, a strong business plan is essential. Here's why:

1. Setting Clear Goals: A business plan helps you define and articulate your business goals. It allows you to establish both short-term and long-term objectives that provide direction and

purpose to your operations. By setting clear and measurable goals, you can track your progress and make informed decisions to drive your business forward.

2. Strategic Planning: A business plan forces you to think strategically about your business. It requires you to assess market conditions, analyze competition, and identify your unique value proposition. Through this process, you can identify opportunities, anticipate challenges, and develop strategies to capitalize on your strengths and mitigate weaknesses. A well-defined strategy helps you make informed decisions and adapt to changing market dynamics.

3. Financial Projections: Business plans include financial projections that outline your revenue, expenses, and profitability over a defined period. These projections help you understand the financial viability of your business and make informed decisions about pricing, cost management, and investment opportunities. Financial projections also play a crucial role in attracting investors or securing financing.

4. Funding and Partnerships: A comprehensive business plan is often required when seeking funding from investors, financial institutions, or potential partners. Investors and lenders need to evaluate the feasibility and potential return on investment of your business. A well-documented business plan provides them with the necessary information to assess the viability of your venture and make informed funding decisions.

5. Operational Efficiency: A business plan helps you establish the operational structure and processes necessary to achieve your goals. It outlines key milestones, timelines, and responsibilities, ensuring that everyone in your organization understands their roles and the overall vision. This clarity promotes efficiency, alignment, and accountability among team members, enabling you to execute your strategies effectively.

6. Risk Management: A business plan allows you to assess potential risks and develop strategies to mitigate them. By conducting a comprehensive analysis of market conditions, competitors, and internal challenges, you can identify potential obstacles and develop contingency plans. This proactive approach helps you anticipate and manage risks, increasing the likelihood of success and resilience in the face of uncertainties.

7. Alignment and Communication: A business plan serves as a communication tool, ensuring that all stakeholders, including

employees, partners, and investors, are aligned around a common vision. It provides a framework to articulate your business model, value proposition, and growth strategies. This alignment fosters teamwork, collaboration, and a shared understanding of the business's direction and objectives.

In conclusion, a well-crafted business plan is a vital document for any entrepreneur. It provides a roadmap, outlines goals and strategies, and communicates the financial viability of your business. Whether you are seeking funding, partnerships, or aligning your team, a strong business plan sets the foundation for success by guiding your decision-making and providing a clear path to achieving your business objectives.

Executive Summary:

The executive summary is a critical component of a business plan, providing a concise overview of your business. It serves as a snapshot that encapsulates the essence of your venture and entices readers to delve deeper into the details. Here's why the executive summary is so important:

1. Concise Overview: The executive summary provides a succinct overview of your business, summarizing its key elements in a clear and concise manner. It introduces the mission, vision, and objectives of your business, giving readers a high-level understanding of what your venture aims to achieve.

2. Mission and Unique Value Proposition: The executive summary highlights your business's mission statement, which communicates the purpose and guiding principles of your organization. It also emphasizes your unique value proposition—the distinctive qualities or advantages that set your business apart from competitors. By articulating your unique value proposition, you capture the attention of readers and establish the relevance and differentiation of your business.

3. Target Market: The executive summary briefly outlines your target market—the specific group of customers or clients you intend to serve. It provides a snapshot of the market segment you are focusing on and highlights the key characteristics and needs of your target audience. This information demonstrates your understanding of the market and helps readers assess the market potential of your business.

4. Competitive Advantage: The executive summary showcases your business's competitive advantage—what sets you apart from other players in the market. It briefly outlines your strengths, such as proprietary technology, unique expertise, strategic partnerships, or superior customer service. By highlighting your competitive advantage, you pique the interest of readers and differentiate your business from competitors.
5. Attention-Grabbing: The executive summary serves as the introduction to your business plan, and its primary purpose is to capture the attention of potential investors or partners. It needs to be compelling, engaging, and concise to hook readers and entice them to continue reading the full plan. A well-crafted executive summary sparks interest, generating enthusiasm and curiosity about your business.
6. Time-Saving: For busy investors or decision-makers, the executive summary serves as a time-saving tool. It provides an at-a-glance view of your business, enabling readers to quickly assess whether your venture aligns with their investment criteria or strategic objectives. If the executive summary resonates with them, they are more likely to invest the time to explore the detailed business plan.
7. Communication and Pitching: The executive summary is also useful for communication purposes, such as networking events or investor pitches. It allows you to concisely articulate your business's value proposition and key highlights, making it easier to communicate your business idea and generate interest in a limited timeframe.

In conclusion, the executive summary is a crucial component of a business plan. It provides a concise overview of your business, highlighting its mission, unique value proposition, target market, and competitive advantage. By capturing the attention of readers and conveying the essence of your business, the executive summary serves as a powerful tool to spark interest, generate enthusiasm, and pave the way for further exploration of your business plan.

Market Analysis:

The market analysis section of a business plan is a crucial component that provides a comprehensive assessment of the industry and market in which your business operates. This section delves into key factors such as market size, growth rates, trends, and competition. Here's why the market analysis is essential:

1. Understanding the Industry: The market analysis helps you gain a deep understanding of the industry in which your business operates. It provides insights into the industry's structure, dynamics, and key players. By examining industry reports, trade publications, and market research data, you can identify industry trends, growth opportunities, and potential challenges. This understanding helps you navigate the industry landscape and make informed decisions.

2. Assessing Market Size and Potential: The market analysis allows you to assess the size and potential of your target market. By analyzing demographic data, customer segmentation, and market research, you can estimate the total addressable market and identify specific market segments to target. Understanding market size helps you assess the revenue potential and attractiveness of your business idea.

3. Identifying Growth Rates and Trends: The market analysis enables you to identify growth rates and trends within your industry. By examining historical data, industry reports, and consumer behavior, you can identify emerging trends, changing consumer preferences, and technological advancements. This insight helps you align your business strategies with market realities, capitalize on opportunities, and stay ahead of the competition.

4. Evaluating Customer Needs and Preferences: Through market analysis, you gain insights into customer needs, preferences, and pain points. This includes analyzing consumer surveys, focus groups, and customer feedback. Understanding customer preferences helps you tailor your products, services, and marketing strategies to meet their specific needs effectively. By aligning your offerings with customer demands, you enhance customer satisfaction and increase your chances of success.

5. Assessing Competitive Landscape: The market analysis involves assessing your competitors and understanding their strengths, weaknesses, and market positioning. By conducting a competitive analysis, you can identify direct and indirect competitors, evaluate their offerings, pricing, and marketing strategies. This analysis helps you identify gaps in the market,

differentiate your business, and develop strategies to gain a competitive edge.

6. Identifying Market Opportunities: The market analysis helps you identify untapped market opportunities and niche segments. By examining market gaps, unmet needs, and underserved customer groups, you can identify areas where your business can offer unique value and gain a competitive advantage. This insight helps you shape your value proposition and develop targeted marketing and sales strategies to capitalize on these opportunities.

7. Positioning Your Business Effectively: The market analysis informs how you position your business in the market. By understanding the competitive landscape, customer needs, and market trends, you can develop a compelling value proposition and unique selling proposition that differentiates your business from competitors. This positioning allows you to attract the right customers, effectively communicate your offerings, and build a strong brand presence.

In conclusion, the market analysis section of a business plan provides a comprehensive assessment of the industry and market in which your business operates. It helps you understand your target audience, identify market opportunities, assess competition, and position your business effectively. By conducting a thorough market analysis, you can make informed decisions, refine your strategies, and increase your chances of success in the marketplace.

Organization and Management Structure:

The organizational structure section of your business plan provides valuable insights into the management and key team members driving your business forward. It outlines the roles, qualifications, expertise, and contributions of your team, showcasing their capabilities and demonstrating a strong and capable management team. Here's why this section is crucial:

1. Demonstrating Expertise: By providing details about the qualifications and expertise of your management team, you demonstrate that you have assembled a capable group of individuals with the necessary skills to drive the success of your business. This instills confidence in investors and partners who want assurance that your team has the knowledge and experience to navigate challenges and make sound decisions.

2. Highlighting Relevant Experience: The organizational structure section allows you to highlight the relevant experience of your team members. This includes their previous roles, accomplishments, and industry-specific expertise. By showcasing their track record and achievements, you establish credibility and assure stakeholders that your team has the necessary know-how to execute your business strategies effectively.

3. Defining Roles and Responsibilities: This section outlines the roles and responsibilities of key team members, providing clarity on the division of tasks and the management structure within your organization. By clearly defining these roles, you establish a framework for accountability and effective collaboration. This structure ensures that each team member understands their responsibilities and contributes to the overall success of the business.

4. Demonstrating Complementary Skill Sets: The organizational structure section allows you to showcase the diverse skill sets of your team members. Highlight how their individual strengths and areas of expertise complement each other, enabling effective teamwork and a well-rounded approach to addressing business challenges. This demonstrates that your team has a comprehensive skill set to tackle various aspects of the business.

5. Inspiring Confidence in Investors and Partners: A strong and capable management team inspires confidence in investors and partners. When potential investors or partners see that your business has a team with the necessary skills, knowledge, and experience to navigate the complexities of the industry, they are more likely to be interested in collaborating or investing in your venture. A competent team strengthens your business's credibility and increases its perceived value.

6. Mitigating Risks: The organizational structure section also helps mitigate risks associated with key personnel. By showcasing a well-rounded team, you minimize the risks of key team members leaving the organization or being unavailable due to unforeseen circumstances. Demonstrating a robust management team reduces the dependence on any single individual and ensures continuity in leadership and decision-making.

7. Attracting Top Talent: In addition to impressing investors and partners, a strong management team highlighted in the organizational structure section can also attract top talent to your organization. Prospective employees are more likely to be attracted to a company that has a capable and experienced leadership team. This can contribute to the recruitment and retention of high-performing individuals who will drive the success of your business.

In conclusion, the organizational structure section of your business plan is vital in showcasing the capabilities and expertise of your management team. By highlighting the qualifications, experience, and contributions of key team members, you inspire confidence in investors, partners, and potential employees. A strong and capable management team instills trust, mitigates risks, and positions your business for success in the marketplace.

Marketing Strategies:

The marketing strategies section of your business plan is crucial in outlining how you will attract and retain customers. It involves identifying your target market segments, selecting appropriate marketing channels, and describing your promotional activities. It also highlights how your marketing efforts align with your overall business goals and how you plan to differentiate yourself from competitors. Here's why this section is important:

1. Target Market Segments: Clearly defining your target market segments is essential for effective marketing. This involves identifying specific groups of customers who are most likely to be interested in your products or services. By understanding their demographics, psychographics, and behaviors, you can tailor your marketing messages and tactics to resonate with each segment. This targeted approach maximizes the effectiveness of your marketing efforts.

2. Marketing Channels: Selecting the right marketing channels is crucial for reaching your target audience. This may include online channels such as social media, search engine marketing, content marketing, and email marketing, as well as offline channels like print advertising, direct mail, and events. Assessing the preferences and behaviors of your target market segments will help you determine the most appropriate channels to engage with and attract customers.

3. Promotional Activities: Describe the promotional activities you will undertake to raise awareness, generate interest, and drive customer acquisition. This may include advertising campaigns, public relations initiatives, content creation, social media engagement, influencer partnerships, and special promotions. Your promotional activities should align with your target market segments and marketing channels to ensure maximum impact.

4. Brand Differentiation: Highlight how your marketing efforts will differentiate your business from competitors. Emphasize your unique value proposition and competitive advantages to position your brand as distinct and appealing to your target audience. This could involve showcasing your superior product features, exceptional customer service, innovative solutions, or sustainability practices. By effectively communicating your differentiators, you create a compelling reason for customers to choose your business over competitors.

5. Integration with Business Goals: Aligning your marketing strategies with your overall business goals is critical for success. Ensure that your marketing efforts are designed to support your broader objectives, such as revenue growth, market expansion, customer retention, or brand recognition. This alignment ensures that your marketing initiatives contribute directly to the achievement of your business goals and drive meaningful results.

6. Measurement and Evaluation: Establish metrics and key performance indicators (KPIs) to measure the effectiveness of your marketing strategies. This could include metrics such as customer acquisition cost, conversion rates, website traffic, social media engagement, and customer satisfaction. Regularly track and evaluate the performance of your marketing activities to make data-driven decisions, optimize your strategies, and refine your approach over time.

7. Continuous Improvement: Emphasize your commitment to continuous improvement and staying updated on marketing trends and best practices. Demonstrate your willingness to adapt and evolve your marketing strategies based on market feedback, customer insights, and changing industry dynamics. This mindset ensures that your marketing efforts remain effective and relevant in an ever-evolving marketplace.

In conclusion, the marketing strategies section of your business plan outlines how you will attract and retain customers. By identifying target market segments, selecting appropriate marketing channels, and describing promotional activities, you create a roadmap for effective marketing. Ensuring alignment with your business goals, differentiating yourself from competitors, and continuously evaluating and improving your marketing efforts will position your business for success and sustainable growth.

Financial Projections:

Financial projections are indeed a critical component of a business plan as they provide a roadmap for the financial performance of your business. They include projected revenue, expenses, and cash flow statements for at least the first three years of operation. These projections are based on realistic assumptions, such as pricing, sales forecasts, and cost estimates. Here's why financial projections are essential and how they are scrutinized by investors and partners:

1. Financial Viability Assessment: Financial projections allow investors and partners to assess the financial viability of your business. By providing a clear picture of expected revenue, expenses, and cash flow, these projections help stakeholders evaluate the potential profitability and sustainability of your venture. They are particularly interested in the projected profitability and the ability of your business to generate positive cash flow.

2. Revenue Projections: Revenue projections outline the expected income generated from the sale of your products or services. They should be based on a realistic assessment of market demand, pricing strategies, and sales forecasts. Investors and partners carefully analyze these projections to gauge the potential revenue growth of your business and assess its ability to generate sufficient income.

3. Expense Projections: Expense projections outline the anticipated costs and expenditures required to operate your business. This includes both fixed costs (such as rent, salaries, and utilities) and variable costs (such as raw materials, marketing expenses, and overhead costs). It is crucial to provide detailed and accurate expense projections to demonstrate your understanding of the costs associated with running your business.

4. Cash Flow Statements: Cash flow projections illustrate the inflows and outflows of cash within your business over a specific period. They help stakeholders assess your business's ability to manage its day-to-day operations, meet financial obligations, and generate positive cash flow. Investors and partners analyze these projections to determine the liquidity and financial health of your business.

5. Realistic Assumptions: Financial projections should be based on realistic assumptions that reflect the current market conditions and industry trends. It is important to provide a transparent and well-supported rationale for your assumptions, such as market research, historical data, or industry benchmarks. Investors and partners scrutinize these assumptions to assess the accuracy and reliability of your projections.

6. Sensitivity Analysis: Conducting sensitivity analysis on your financial projections demonstrates your understanding of the potential risks and uncertainties associated with your business. This analysis involves assessing how changes in key variables, such as sales volumes, pricing, or production costs, can impact your financial performance. Investors and partners value this analysis as it shows that you have considered various scenarios and have contingency plans in place.

7. Profitability and Return on Investment: Investors and partners pay close attention to the projected profitability and return on investment (ROI) of your business. They analyze the net profit margins, gross margins, and other profitability ratios to assess the potential return they can expect from their investment. Providing well-supported financial projections helps instill confidence in stakeholders regarding the financial viability and potential growth of your business.

In conclusion, financial projections are a crucial aspect of a business plan as they provide stakeholders with a clear understanding of the expected financial performance of your business. By including revenue projections, expense projections, and cash flow statements, you demonstrate the financial viability and sustainability of your venture. Investors and partners scrutinize these projections, looking for realistic assumptions, profitability, and return on investment potential. Providing accurate and well-supported financial projections is vital to instill confidence and secure the support needed for your business's success.

Contingency Plans:

Contingency plans play a crucial role in addressing potential risks and challenges that may impact your business. By identifying key risks, such as economic downturns, regulatory changes, or supply chain disruptions, and outlining strategies to mitigate those risks, you demonstrate foresight and preparedness. Here's why contingency planning is important and how it contributes to your business's success:

1. Risk Identification: Contingency planning begins with identifying potential risks that could adversely affect your business. This involves conducting a thorough risk assessment, considering internal and external factors that could impact your operations, finances, or market positioning. By proactively identifying risks, you can take proactive measures to mitigate their potential impact.

2. Risk Mitigation Strategies: Once risks are identified, contingency planning involves developing strategies to minimize their impact on your business. This may include diversifying your customer base or supplier network, implementing robust financial management practices, securing appropriate insurance coverage, or maintaining strong relationships with regulatory authorities. These strategies help reduce the vulnerability of your business to potential risks.

3. Preparedness for Uncertain Circumstances: Contingency planning prepares your business to navigate uncertain circumstances with agility and resilience. By considering various scenarios and outlining response strategies, you are better equipped to adapt to unexpected changes in the business environment. This preparedness enables you to make informed decisions, minimize disruptions, and maintain business continuity even during challenging times.

4. Stakeholder Confidence: Having well-defined contingency plans demonstrates your commitment to risk management and instills confidence in stakeholders, including investors, lenders, and partners. It shows that you have considered potential challenges and have strategies in place to mitigate them. This level of preparedness increases trust and enhances your business's reputation.

5. Regulatory Compliance: Contingency planning helps ensure compliance with regulatory requirements. By anticipating potential regulatory changes and developing strategies to

adapt, you can minimize the impact of new regulations on your business. This proactive approach demonstrates your commitment to adhering to legal and regulatory frameworks and reduces the risk of non-compliance.

6. Business Continuity: Contingency planning is essential for maintaining business continuity during unforeseen events or crises. It enables you to respond swiftly and effectively, minimizing disruptions to your operations and customer service. By having well-defined contingency plans, you can navigate through challenging circumstances and emerge stronger on the other side.

7. Continuous Improvement: Contingency planning is an ongoing process that should be regularly reviewed and updated as your business evolves. As you gain new insights, experience, and market knowledge, you can refine your contingency plans to align with emerging risks and opportunities. This continuous improvement mindset ensures that your business remains adaptable and resilient in an ever-changing business landscape.

In conclusion, contingency planning is a vital aspect of business planning that addresses potential risks and challenges. By identifying risks, developing strategies to mitigate them, and being prepared for uncertain circumstances, you position your business for success. Contingency planning instills stakeholder confidence, ensures regulatory compliance, enables business continuity, and fosters a culture of continuous improvement. By embracing the planning process and investing time and effort into developing robust contingency plans, you strengthen your business's ability to navigate uncertainties and thrive in a dynamic marketplace.

Securing financing and funding options:

Starting a business indeed often requires a capital investment, and exploring the various financing options available in Florida is crucial to secure the necessary funds. Here are some financing options to consider:

Traditional Bank Loans:

Traditional bank loans are indeed a common and widely accessible option for small businesses seeking financing. These loans typically involve a formal application process, collateral requirements, and a structured repayment schedule. Here's why traditional bank loans are a popular choice and what you need to consider when applying for one:

1. Accessible Financing: Traditional bank loans provide small businesses with access to capital to support their growth and operations. Banks have established lending programs and resources dedicated to assisting small businesses, making it easier for entrepreneurs to secure the funding they need.

2. Application Process: Applying for a traditional bank loan involves submitting a loan application that typically requires detailed information about your business, including its financials, projected cash flow, and business plan. Banks will also consider your credit history and personal financial information during the evaluation process. It is important to prepare a comprehensive and well-documented loan application to increase your chances of approval.

3. Collateral Requirements: Banks often require collateral to secure the loan. Collateral can be in the form of assets, such as real estate, inventory, or equipment, which the bank can seize and sell in the event of default. Collateral provides a level of assurance for the bank and may affect the loan terms and interest rates offered.

4. Repayment Structure: Traditional bank loans typically have a structured repayment schedule with fixed monthly installments over a set period. The terms and interest rates of the loan will depend on factors such as your creditworthiness, business financials, and collateral offered. It is crucial to carefully review and understand the repayment terms to ensure that they align with your business's cash flow capabilities.

5. Comprehensive Business Plan: To increase your chances of approval for a traditional bank loan, it is important to prepare a comprehensive business plan that outlines your business model, market analysis, financial projections, and growth strategies. A well-documented business plan demonstrates your preparedness, knowledge, and commitment to the success of your business.

6. Financial Statements: Banks typically require financial statements, including income statements, balance sheets, and cash flow statements, to assess your business's financial health and repayment capacity. It is essential to maintain accurate and up-to-date financial records to support your loan application.

7. Credit History: Your personal and business credit history will play a significant role in the bank's evaluation of your loan application. A strong credit history demonstrates your ability to manage debt responsibly and increases your chances of loan approval. It is important to monitor and maintain good credit practices to enhance your creditworthiness.

In conclusion, traditional bank loans are a viable financing option for small businesses. To increase your chances of approval, it is crucial to prepare a comprehensive loan application that includes a well-documented business plan, financial statements, and a strong credit history. Understanding the application process, collateral requirements, and repayment structure will help you navigate the loan process effectively and secure the financing you need to support your business's growth and operations.

Small Business Administration (SBA) Loans:

The Small Business Administration (SBA) offers various loan programs specifically designed to support and assist small businesses. These SBA loans are known for providing more favorable terms compared to traditional bank loans, making them an attractive financing option for entrepreneurs. Here's why SBA loans are beneficial and how they work:

1. Favorable Terms: SBA loans typically offer more favorable terms, including lower down payments, longer repayment periods, and lower interest rates compared to traditional bank loans. These terms are designed to support small businesses and make loan repayment more manageable.
2. Loan Programs: The SBA offers multiple loan programs to cater to different business needs. The most popular SBA loan program is the 7(a) Loan Program, which provides general-purpose loans for working capital, equipment purchase, and business acquisition. Other programs, such as the CDC/504 Loan Program and the Microloan Program, focus on specific needs such as real estate or small-dollar loans.
3. Partner Lenders: The SBA works with a network of approved lenders, including banks and credit unions, to facilitate the loan process. These partner lenders provide the funds, while the SBA guarantees a portion of the loan, reducing the risk for the lenders. This guarantee mitigates some of the lender's concerns and encourages them to provide financing to small businesses that may not qualify for traditional bank loans.

4. Application Process: Applying for an SBA loan involves working with an SBA-approved lender. The lender evaluates your loan application based on their own criteria as well as SBA guidelines. The SBA loan application typically requires detailed information about your business, financial statements, business plan, and personal financial information.

5. Collateral Requirements: While SBA loans generally require collateral, the SBA's loan guarantee can help reduce the collateral requirements compared to traditional bank loans. The specific collateral requirements may vary depending on the loan program and the lender's policies.

6. Support and Resources: The SBA provides support and resources to help small businesses navigate the loan application process. They offer guidance, workshops, and online tools to assist entrepreneurs in understanding the loan programs, eligibility requirements, and documentation needed.

7. Assistance for Special Situations: The SBA also offers loan programs tailored to specific situations, such as disaster assistance loans for businesses affected by natural disasters or economic injury disaster loans for businesses facing temporary financial hardship.

In conclusion, SBA loans are a valuable financing option for small businesses, offering more favorable terms compared to traditional bank loans. The SBA works with partner lenders to facilitate the loan process and mitigate risk, making it easier for small businesses to access the funding they need. Understanding the various SBA loan programs, their terms, and the application process can help you take advantage of these resources to support your business's growth and success.

Grants:

Grants are indeed a valuable source of funding for small businesses as they provide non-repayable funds to support various business activities. Grants are typically offered by government agencies, foundations, or organizations and are awarded based on specific criteria. Here's why grants are beneficial and how to approach them:

1. Non-Repayable Funding: Grants provide small businesses with financial resources without the burden of repayment. Unlike loans, grants do not need to be paid back, allowing businesses to invest in growth and development without incurring debt.

2. Funding for Specific Purposes: Grants often target specific purposes or areas of focus, such as research and development, environmental sustainability, innovation, or community development. By identifying grants relevant to your business, you can align your funding needs with the specific objectives and requirements of grant programs.

3. Government Agencies, Foundations, and Organizations: Grants are offered by various entities, including government agencies at the federal, state, and local levels, private foundations, and non-profit organizations. Researching and identifying the right grant opportunities requires a thorough understanding of these entities and their funding priorities.

4. Eligibility and Criteria: Each grant program has specific eligibility requirements and criteria that must be met for consideration. These criteria may include business type, location, industry focus, stage of development, social impact, or specific project objectives. Carefully review the eligibility requirements to ensure that your business meets the necessary criteria before investing time and effort in the application process.

5. Application Process: Applying for grants typically involves a formal application process that requires submitting detailed information about your business, project plans, financial statements, and supporting documents. The application process may also involve writing a compelling proposal that effectively communicates the purpose, goals, and expected outcomes of your project.

6. Competition and Evaluation: Grant programs often receive a high volume of applications, making the competition for funding intense. Your application will be evaluated based on the merit of your proposal, alignment with the grant program's objectives, and the potential impact of your project. Craft a strong application that clearly demonstrates the value and feasibility of your project.

7. Reporting and Accountability: If awarded a grant, you will be required to comply with reporting and accountability requirements. This includes providing progress reports, financial statements, and other documentation to demonstrate the effective use of grant funds and the achievement of project goals. It is crucial to maintain accurate records and fulfill the reporting obligations outlined by the grant program.

In conclusion, grants offer non-repayable funding to support small businesses in various areas of focus. By researching and identifying relevant grant opportunities, carefully reviewing eligibility requirements, and submitting a compelling application, you can increase your chances of securing grant funding. Remember to comply with reporting and accountability requirements if awarded a grant. Grants can provide a valuable financial boost to your business and support specific projects or initiatives that align with the objectives of grant programs.

Venture Capital:

Venture capital is indeed a funding option that involves obtaining capital from investors in exchange for equity or ownership in your business. Venture capital is often sought by businesses with high-growth potential, particularly in technology, innovation, or scalable industries. Here's what you need to know about venture capital and how it works:

1. Capital in Exchange for Equity: Venture capitalists provide capital to businesses in exchange for an ownership stake. This means that the venture capitalist becomes a shareholder and shares in the future profits and growth of the business. The percentage of equity acquired by the venture capitalist is typically negotiated based on the valuation and potential of the business.

2. High-Growth Potential Businesses: Venture capital is more suitable for businesses with significant growth potential. Venture capitalists are particularly interested in businesses that offer innovative products or services, disruptive technologies, or scalable business models. These businesses have the potential to generate substantial returns on investment within a relatively short timeframe.

3. Active Involvement and Support: Venture capitalists often provide more than just funding. They bring expertise, industry connections, and mentorship to help businesses grow and succeed. They may actively participate in the management and strategic decision-making processes, providing valuable guidance and support.

4. Risk and Return: Venture capitalists take on higher risks by investing in early-stage or high-growth businesses. They seek a significant return on their investment to compensate for this

risk. Venture capitalists expect the businesses they invest in to achieve rapid growth, generate substantial revenue, and ultimately provide an exit opportunity, such as an initial public offering (IPO) or acquisition.

5. Due Diligence Process: Venture capitalists conduct thorough due diligence before investing in a business. This involves assessing the business model, market potential, competitive landscape, management team, financials, and growth strategy. They carefully evaluate the potential risks and rewards associated with the investment.

6. Funding Rounds: Venture capital funding often occurs in multiple rounds, starting with seed funding and progressing to later-stage rounds as the business grows and achieves milestones. Each funding round provides additional capital to support the business's expansion and development.

7. Exit Strategy: Venture capitalists typically have a specific exit strategy in mind when investing. They seek to realize their return on investment by selling their equity stake in the business. This may occur through an IPO, acquisition by another company, or a secondary market sale.

It is important to note that venture capital may not be suitable for every business. Venture capitalists are highly selective and invest in businesses with exceptional growth potential. If your business aligns with the criteria and objectives of venture capital investors, seeking venture capital funding can provide significant financial resources, expertise, and industry connections to propel your business's growth and success.

Angel Investors:

Angel investors play a crucial role in funding early-stage businesses and supporting their growth. These individuals are typically high-net-worth individuals who invest their personal funds in promising ventures. Here's what you need to know about angel investors and how they can benefit your business:

1. Personal Funding: Angel investors provide personal funds to early-stage businesses, offering financial support when traditional bank loans or other funding sources may be challenging to secure. Their investments can provide the necessary capital to fuel business growth, develop products or services, expand operations, or enter new markets.

2. Mentorship and Expertise: In addition to financial support, angel investors often bring valuable industry expertise, mentorship, and guidance. They may have a background in your industry and can provide insights, advice, and strategic direction based on their own experiences. This mentorship can be invaluable in helping you navigate challenges, make informed decisions, and avoid common pitfalls.

3. Networking Opportunities: Angel investors often have extensive networks within their industry or business community. They can introduce you to potential customers, partners, suppliers, or other investors who can further support your business growth. Leveraging their network can provide valuable connections and open doors to new opportunities.

4. Strategic Support: Angel investors may actively participate in the management and strategic decision-making of the business. They may offer their expertise to help refine business models, fine-tune marketing strategies, or enhance operational efficiency. Their involvement can contribute to the overall growth and success of the business.

5. Equity or Convertible Debt: Angel investors typically invest in exchange for equity ownership or convertible debt. Equity investment involves the angel investor becoming a shareholder in your business, sharing in the future profits and growth. Convertible debt is a loan that can convert into equity under specified conditions, such as a future funding round or milestone achievement.

6. Early-Stage Investment: Angel investors are often interested in innovative and high-potential ventures in their early stages. They are willing to take on higher risks associated with early-stage businesses in exchange for the potential for significant returns on their investment. Their investment can provide the necessary capital to validate your business concept, build traction, and attract further funding.

7. Due Diligence Process: Angel investors conduct due diligence before investing in a business. They evaluate factors such as the market potential, competitive landscape, management team, financials, and growth strategy. This process helps them assess the viability and potential of the business before making an investment decision.

When seeking angel investment, it is crucial to present a compelling business case, demonstrate market potential, and highlight how the investment aligns with your business's growth plans. Establishing a mutually beneficial relationship based on trust, open communication, and aligned objectives is key to maximizing the value that angel investors can bring to your business.

In conclusion, angel investors provide personal funds, mentorship, industry expertise, and networking opportunities to early-stage businesses. Their investment can fuel growth, while their guidance and support can contribute to the overall success of your business. Understanding the motivations and expectations of angel investors and effectively articulating the value proposition of your business are essential in attracting their interest and securing their investment.

Crowdfunding:

Crowdfunding has emerged as a popular alternative financing option for entrepreneurs seeking capital to support their business ventures. Crowdfunding platforms allow you to present your business idea or product to a broad audience and invite individuals to contribute funds. Here's what you need to know about crowdfunding and how it can benefit your business:

1. Access to a Large Pool of Potential Investors: Crowdfunding platforms provide access to a large community of potential investors, supporters, and customers who are interested in innovative ideas and entrepreneurial ventures. By showcasing your business on these platforms, you can attract contributions from individuals who resonate with your vision and value proposition.

2. Financial Support: Crowdfunding can provide the necessary funds to launch or expand your business. Contributions can come from a large number of individuals, each providing a small amount, which collectively adds up to a significant sum. This decentralized approach to fundraising can be especially beneficial for entrepreneurs who may struggle to secure financing through traditional means.

3. Market Validation: Crowdfunding campaigns not only provide financial support but also offer market validation. When individuals contribute to your campaign, they are essentially signaling their interest in and support for your business idea or product. This validation can be valuable in attracting further

investment or gaining the attention of potential partners, customers, or distributors.

4. Engagement and Customer Base: Crowdfunding allows you to engage directly with your supporters and build a community around your business. By involving your contributors in the process, sharing updates, and offering rewards or perks, you can foster a sense of loyalty and create a base of early adopters for your product or service.

5. Pre-selling Opportunities: Some crowdfunding models, such as reward-based crowdfunding, allow you to offer your product or service as a reward for contributions. This provides an opportunity to generate pre-sales and gauge market demand before fully launching your product or service.

6. Market Exposure and Publicity: Crowdfunding campaigns often attract media attention and can generate buzz around your business. This exposure can increase awareness, generate publicity, and attract potential customers, investors, or partners who discover your business through the crowdfunding platform.

7. Crowdfunding Models: There are different crowdfunding models, including rewards-based crowdfunding, equity crowdfunding, and donation-based crowdfunding. Each model has its own considerations, such as offering rewards or equity in exchange for contributions. Carefully evaluate the different models and choose the one that aligns best with your business goals and funding needs.

When considering crowdfunding as a financing option, it is important to thoroughly plan and execute your campaign. This includes developing a compelling pitch, setting realistic funding goals, preparing engaging content and visuals, and effectively leveraging your networks and social media platforms to promote your campaign.

While crowdfunding can be a viable source of funding, it is essential to understand the potential challenges and limitations. Competition on crowdfunding platforms is intense, and successfully attracting contributions requires a well-executed campaign and a compelling value proposition.

In conclusion, crowdfunding offers entrepreneurs an alternative means of financing their business ventures, providing not only financial support but also market validation, customer engagement, and publicity. By leveraging crowdfunding platforms effectively and engaging with supporters, you can access the resources needed to launch and grow your business successfully.

Identifying target customers and competition:

Understanding your target customers is a crucial aspect of building a successful business. By defining your ideal customer profile, you can gain valuable insights into their demographics, behaviors, needs, and preferences. This understanding allows you to tailor your products or services, marketing messages, and customer experiences to effectively meet their expectations.

To define your ideal customer profile, conduct market research, analyze customer data, and engage in customer feedback and surveys. This will help you identify key characteristics such as age, gender, location, income level, and interests. By segmenting your target audience, you can develop targeted marketing strategies that resonate with specific customer groups.

Once you have a clear understanding of your target customers, it's essential to conduct a competitive analysis. This involves studying your competitors' products, pricing strategies, marketing tactics, and customer feedback. By analyzing their strengths and weaknesses, you can identify opportunities for differentiation and develop strategies to gain a competitive advantage.

During the competitive analysis, consider factors such as market share, unique selling propositions, customer reviews, brand reputation, and pricing. Assess the gaps in the market that your business can fill, identify unmet customer needs, and determine how your products or services can provide superior value.

Furthermore, identify your own strengths and differentiators. Determine what sets your business apart from competitors and articulate your unique value proposition. This could be factors such as quality, innovation, customer service, or convenience. Highlighting these differentiators in your marketing messages and customer interactions will help you stand out in the marketplace.

As you develop your marketing strategies, ensure they align with your target customer profile and competitive analysis. Tailor your messaging, branding, and promotional activities to effectively reach and engage your target audience. Utilize various marketing channels, such as digital advertising, social media, content marketing, and targeted promotions, to reach your customers where they are most likely to be.

Regularly monitor and evaluate the effectiveness of your marketing strategies and adjust them as needed. Stay updated on market trends, customer preferences, and changes in the competitive landscape to remain agile and responsive to market dynamics.

In conclusion, understanding your target customers and analyzing your competition are fundamental to building a successful business. By defining your ideal customer profile and conducting a thorough competitive analysis, you can develop targeted marketing strategies and differentiate your business in the marketplace. Continuously monitor and adapt your strategies to stay relevant and effectively meet the evolving needs of your customers.

Establishing a strong brand identity:

Creating a strong brand identity is indeed crucial for attracting customers and establishing credibility in the marketplace. A well-defined brand helps differentiate your business from competitors and connects with your target audience on an emotional level. Here's how you can develop a compelling brand identity:

1. Brand Message: Craft a clear and compelling brand message that communicates the unique value your business offers. This message should encapsulate your mission, vision, and the benefits customers can expect from your products or services. It should resonate with your target audience and differentiate your business in the marketplace.
2. Company Name: Choose a company name that reflects your brand personality, values, and target audience. Consider factors such as memorability, relevance, and the availability of domain names and trademarks. Ensure that your company name aligns with your brand message and creates a positive association in the minds of your customers.
3. Logo and Visual Elements: Design a visually appealing and distinctive logo that captures the essence of your brand. Your logo should be memorable, versatile, and reflective of your brand's personality. Consider colors, fonts, and graphical elements that convey the desired brand attributes and evoke the desired emotional response from your audience.

4. Tagline: Develop a concise and impactful tagline that summarizes your brand promise and communicates a key benefit or value proposition. A well-crafted tagline can leave a lasting impression and reinforce your brand message in the minds of your customers.

5. Consistency: Consistently apply your brand identity across all marketing channels and touchpoints. This includes your website, social media profiles, packaging, advertising materials, and customer communications. Consistency in visual elements, tone of voice, and brand messaging helps establish recognition and builds trust with your target audience.

6. Brand Personality and Voice: Define your brand personality and voice, which will guide how you communicate and interact with your audience. Consider the emotions and qualities you want your brand to evoke, whether it's friendly, professional, innovative, or trustworthy. Ensure that your brand personality aligns with your target audience's preferences and aspirations.

7. Brand Experience: Create a consistent and memorable brand experience for your customers. This includes every interaction they have with your business, from the moment they discover your brand to post-purchase support. Deliver on your brand promise and consistently provide exceptional products, services, and customer experiences that align with your brand values.

Building a strong brand identity takes time, consistency, and a deep understanding of your target audience. Regularly monitor and evaluate how your brand is perceived and make adjustments as necessary to ensure it remains relevant and resonates with your customers.

In conclusion, creating a strong brand identity is essential for attracting customers and building credibility. By developing a compelling brand message, designing impactful visual elements, and consistently applying your brand across all touchpoints, you can establish recognition and trust among your target audience. Stay true to your brand values and consistently deliver exceptional experiences to build long-term relationships with your customers.

Setting realistic goals and objectives:

Setting clear goals and objectives is indeed essential for guiding your business and measuring progress. Here's how you can effectively establish goals that align with your overall business vision:

1. Vision and Mission: Start by defining your business's vision and mission. Your vision is the long-term aspiration you have for your business, while your mission outlines the purpose and value you provide to customers. These foundational elements will guide the goals you set and help keep your business on track.
2. Short-Term and Long-Term Goals: Develop both short-term and long-term goals that support your vision and mission. Short-term goals focus on immediate targets and can help you track progress more frequently, while long-term goals outline milestones you aim to achieve over a more extended period. Having a combination of both provides a balanced perspective and ensures progress towards your larger objectives.
3. SMART Goals: Ensure that your goals are SMART—specific, measurable, achievable, relevant, and time-bound. Specific goals clearly define what you want to accomplish, measurable goals allow you to track progress and determine success, achievable goals are realistic and attainable, relevant goals align with your overall business objectives, and time-bound goals have a specific timeframe for completion.
4. Prioritization: Prioritize your goals based on their significance and impact on your business. Identify the most critical goals that will have the greatest influence on your success and focus your efforts on those. This will help you allocate resources effectively and make progress towards your most important objectives.
5. Regular Evaluation and Adjustment: Regularly evaluate your goals and assess your progress. This allows you to identify areas where you may need to adjust your strategies or resources. Business conditions and market dynamics can change, so it's important to remain flexible and adapt your goals as needed to stay aligned with your vision and respond to new opportunities or challenges.
6. Communication and Alignment: Share your goals with your team and stakeholders, ensuring everyone understands and is aligned with the direction of the business. Clear communication fosters a sense of shared purpose and encourages collaboration towards achieving the goals.
7. Celebrate Milestones: Celebrate milestones and achievements along the way. Recognize and reward progress to motivate

yourself and your team, boosting morale and maintaining momentum as you work towards your larger goals.

Regularly revisit and review your goals, making adjustments as necessary. This ongoing process of setting, evaluating, and adjusting goals ensures your business stays on track, adapts to changing circumstances, and remains focused on achieving long-term success.

In conclusion, setting clear goals and objectives is crucial for guiding your business and measuring progress. By defining specific, measurable, achievable, relevant, and time-bound goals that align with your vision and mission, you establish a roadmap for success. Regularly evaluate and adjust your goals as your business evolves, and communicate them effectively to foster alignment and engagement within your team. With a clear focus on your goals, you are well-positioned to navigate the competitive business landscape and achieve success in Florida.

Chapter 2:

Registering Your Business in Florida

Registering your business in Florida is a critical step in establishing your legal presence and ensuring compliance with state and local regulations. This chapter will guide you through the essential elements of the registration process.

Choosing and registering a business name:

Selecting a unique and memorable business name is indeed a crucial step in establishing your brand identity. Here's a guide to help you navigate the process:

1. Conduct a Comprehensive Search: Before finalizing your business name, conduct a thorough search to ensure it is not already in use by another entity. Start by searching online directories, business registries, and social media platforms. Check for any existing trademarks or domain names that could create confusion or legal issues.
2. Register Your Business Name: Once you've confirmed the availability of your chosen name, it is advisable to register it with the Florida Department of State. Registering your business name helps establish legal rights and prevents others from using the same name within the state. The registration process typically involves filing the appropriate forms and paying the required fees.
3. Consider Trademark Protection: While registering your business name with the state offers some level of protection, it is also important to consider trademark protection. A trademark provides broader legal protection, preventing others from using a similar name or logo that could create confusion among consumers. Consulting with an attorney experienced in intellectual property law can help you navigate the trademark registration process and ensure proper protection for your brand.
4. Perform a Trademark Search: Before finalizing your business name, conduct a thorough trademark search to determine if there are existing trademarks that may conflict with your chosen name. This search can be conducted through the United States Patent and Trademark Office (USPTO) database or by

engaging the services of a trademark attorney or professional search firm.

5. Consult with an Attorney: Engaging an attorney who specializes in intellectual property law can provide valuable guidance throughout the naming and trademark registration process. An attorney can help you understand the legal implications, advise on potential conflicts, and ensure compliance with trademark laws.

6. Protect Your Online Presence: In addition to selecting a business name, secure relevant domain names for your website and social media handles associated with your brand. This helps ensure consistency across digital platforms and prevents others from using your chosen name in the online space.

By conducting a comprehensive search, registering your business name, and considering trademark protection, you establish a strong foundation for your brand identity. It is crucial to prioritize legal compliance and protect your business name from potential conflicts or infringements. Working with legal professionals can provide the expertise needed to navigate any complex issues and safeguard your brand's reputation and intellectual property.

Remember, selecting a unique and legally protected business name not only differentiates your business in the marketplace but also establishes a strong and memorable brand identity that resonates with your target audience.

Registering for a Federal Employer Identification Number (FEIN):

Obtaining a Federal Employer Identification Number (FEIN) is indeed a crucial step for businesses that plan to hire employees, operate as a partnership or corporation, or have other tax obligations. Here's what you need to know about applying for an FEIN:

1. Determine if You Need an FEIN: Evaluate your business structure and tax obligations to determine if you need an FEIN. Businesses that have employees, operate as a partnership or corporation, or meet other criteria outlined by the IRS generally require an FEIN.

2. Free Application Process: Applying for an FEIN is free, and you can do so online or by mail. The online application process is typically faster and more convenient. Alternatively, you can complete Form SS-4, Application for Employer Identification

Number, and submit it by mail or fax to the appropriate IRS office.

3. Gather Required Information: Before applying for an FEIN, gather the necessary information for the application. This may include your business name, address, structure, ownership details, and the responsible party's personal information (such as their name and Social Security Number or Individual Taxpayer Identification Number).

4. Online Application Process: To apply online, visit the IRS website and navigate to the "Apply for an Employer Identification Number (EIN) Online" section. Follow the prompts and provide the required information. Once you submit the application, you will receive an EIN immediately.

5. Mail Application Process: If you prefer to apply by mail, complete Form SS-4 with accurate and complete information. Review the instructions provided with the form to ensure you include all necessary details. Mail the completed form to the appropriate IRS office as indicated in the instructions. It may take several weeks to receive your EIN by mail.

6. Use Your FEIN for Tax and Legal Purposes: Once you obtain your FEIN, it becomes a unique identifier for your business entity. You will use it for various tax and legal purposes, including filing tax returns, reporting employee wages, and conducting business transactions. Ensure that you keep your FEIN secure and use it responsibly.

Obtaining an FEIN is a necessary step to ensure compliance with federal tax regulations and establish your business's identity for tax and legal purposes. It is important to apply for an FEIN promptly and accurately to avoid delays in your business operations and potential penalties.

If you have questions or need assistance during the application process, consult with a tax professional or contact the IRS directly for guidance.

3. Applying for state and local business licenses:

Complying with state and local licensing requirements is crucial for operating your business legally in Florida. Depending on your industry and location, you may need specific licenses or permits to ensure compliance with regulations. Here are the steps to follow when researching and obtaining the necessary licenses or permits:

1. Determine Applicable Licensing Requirements: Research and identify the specific licenses or permits required for your industry and location in Florida. The licensing requirements can vary depending on factors such as the nature of your business, the services you provide, and the location where you operate.
2. Contact Relevant Agencies: Reach out to the appropriate state and local government agencies responsible for issuing licenses and permits in your industry. These agencies may include the Florida Department of Business and Professional Regulation (DBPR), local city or county licensing departments, or specialized regulatory boards.
3. Understand Application Procedures: Familiarize yourself with the application procedures, documentation requirements, and any associated fees for obtaining the required licenses or permits. Each licensing agency may have specific guidelines and forms that need to be completed, so ensure that you gather the necessary information and prepare the required documentation.
4. Complete the Application Process: Follow the instructions provided by the licensing agency and complete the application process accurately and thoroughly. Provide all requested information, supporting documents, and any additional requirements specified by the agency.
5. Compliance with Additional Requirements: In addition to obtaining licenses or permits, be aware of any additional compliance requirements specific to your industry. This may include maintaining professional certifications, meeting ongoing education or training requirements, or adhering to specific standards or regulations.
6. Renewal and Ongoing Compliance: Once you have obtained the necessary licenses or permits, it is important to stay informed about renewal procedures and deadlines. Many licenses and permits require periodic renewal, and failure to renew on time could result in penalties or the loss of your license. Stay updated on any changes to licensing requirements or regulations that may impact your business.

Remember that licensing requirements can vary depending on your industry, so it is crucial to research and understand the specific requirements that apply to your business. Consulting with an attorney or industry-specific associations can provide valuable guidance and ensure that you fulfill all necessary licensing obligations.

By complying with state and local licensing requirements, you demonstrate your commitment to operating your business legally and ethically. It also helps build trust with customers and provides assurance that you meet the necessary standards to deliver your products or services.

Understanding sales tax and permits:

If your business involves selling tangible goods or certain services in Florida, registering for a sales tax number is a crucial step to ensure compliance with state tax regulations. Here's what you need to know about registering for a Florida sales tax number:

1. Determine Your Sales Tax Obligations: Assess whether your business activities require the collection and remittance of sales tax. Generally, businesses that sell tangible goods or certain taxable services are required to register for a sales tax number in Florida.

2. Register with the Florida Department of Revenue: To obtain a sales tax number, you will need to register with the Florida Department of Revenue (DOR). You can register online through the DOR's website or by submitting a paper application. Provide accurate information about your business activities, including the type of products or services you sell.

3. Collecting and Remitting Sales Tax: Once you have your sales tax number, you are responsible for collecting sales tax from customers at the applicable rate and remitting it to the Florida DOR. Ensure that you understand the sales tax rates applicable to your specific products or services, as they may vary.

4. Additional Permits or Licenses: Depending on the nature of your business, you may require additional permits or licenses related to sales tax. For example, if you operate a restaurant or sell alcoholic beverages, you may need special permits or licenses in addition to your sales tax number. Research the specific requirements for your industry and comply with any additional obligations.

5. Sales Tax Reporting and Filing: As a registered business, you will be required to file regular sales tax returns with the Florida DOR. These returns report the sales tax collected from customers and calculate the amount owed to the state. Ensure

that you understand the filing deadlines and reporting requirements to avoid penalties or interest charges.

6. Stay Updated on Sales Tax Changes: Sales tax regulations and rates may change over time, so it is important to stay updated on any updates or revisions by regularly checking the Florida DOR's website or subscribing to their notifications. This ensures that you remain compliant with the latest requirements.

7. Consult with a Tax Professional: If you have any questions or need guidance regarding sales tax registration, collection, or reporting, consider consulting with a tax professional or accountant who specializes in Florida tax regulations. They can provide valuable advice tailored to your specific business situation.

By registering for a sales tax number and fulfilling your sales tax obligations, you demonstrate your commitment to complying with Florida tax laws and contribute to the funding of essential government services. Adhering to sales tax requirements helps maintain the integrity of the tax system and avoids potential penalties or legal consequences.

Complying with zoning and land use regulations:

Complying with zoning and land use regulations is indeed essential for businesses to operate legally and avoid potential legal complications. Here's a guide to help you navigate zoning requirements for your business:

1. Research Zoning Regulations: Familiarize yourself with the zoning regulations and land use requirements specific to your intended business location. Zoning regulations dictate how land can be used and designate specific areas for residential, commercial, industrial, or mixed-use purposes. Research the zoning codes, ordinances, and maps established by the local government or planning department.

2. Determine Permitted Uses: Identify the permitted uses within the designated zone where you plan to establish your business. Each zone has its own set of allowed uses, such as retail, office, industrial, or residential. Ensure that your business activities align with the permitted uses for the specific zone in which you intend to operate.

3. Consult with Local Authorities: Reach out to the local planning department or zoning board to clarify any questions you may

have regarding the zoning requirements. They can provide guidance on whether your proposed business activities comply with the zoning regulations and if any special permits or variances are required.

4. Special Use Permits or Variances: In some cases, your business activities may not be explicitly permitted within a specific zone but could qualify for a special use permit or variance. These permits allow for exceptions to the zoning regulations, permitting specific uses on a case-by-case basis. Consult with local authorities or an attorney to determine if your business qualifies for such permits and understand the application process.

5. Seek Legal Counsel: If you encounter complex zoning issues or require assistance navigating the zoning process, consider consulting with an attorney specializing in land use and zoning regulations. An attorney can review your specific circumstances, advise you on the applicable zoning requirements, and guide you through the necessary steps to ensure compliance.

6. Consider Future Growth and Expansion: When selecting a business location, consider the potential for future growth and expansion. Evaluate zoning regulations to determine if they allow for the scalability of your business or if they may impose limitations on future development. This forward-thinking approach can help you avoid potential obstacles as your business evolves.

7. Community Engagement: Engaging with the local community and stakeholders can help build support for your business and address any concerns related to zoning. Participate in community meetings, engage in open dialogue with neighbors, and demonstrate your commitment to being a responsible and compatible member of the community.

By understanding and complying with zoning and land use regulations, you ensure that your business operates within the parameters set by local authorities. This not only helps you avoid potential legal challenges but also fosters a positive relationship with the community and contributes to the overall development and vitality of the area.

Remember, zoning regulations can vary significantly from one location to another, so thorough research and consultation with local authorities or legal professionals are essential to ensure compliance with the specific requirements applicable to your business.

Registering trademarks and copyrights:

Protecting your intellectual property is crucial for maintaining the uniqueness and value of your business. Here are key steps to consider when safeguarding your intellectual assets:

1. Trademark Registration: If you have unique branding elements, such as logos, slogans, or product names, consider registering them as trademarks with the United States Patent and Trademark Office (USPTO). Trademarks provide exclusive rights to use and protect your brand identity, preventing others from using similar marks in a way that could cause confusion among consumers. Registering your trademarks strengthens your legal protection and allows you to take legal action against infringers.

2. Copyright Protection: Copyright law protects original creative works, such as literary, artistic, or musical creations. If you have original content, such as written materials, designs, artwork, or software, you may consider obtaining copyright protection. Although copyright protection exists automatically upon creation, registering your copyright with the U.S. Copyright Office provides additional benefits, such as the ability to sue for infringement and claim statutory damages.

3. Conduct Intellectual Property Searches: Before registering trademarks or seeking copyright protection, it is essential to conduct comprehensive searches to ensure that your intellectual assets do not infringe on existing rights. This involves searching the USPTO database, copyright databases, and other relevant sources to identify potentially conflicting trademarks or copyrighted works. Consulting an intellectual property attorney can help you navigate the search process effectively.

4. Work with an Intellectual Property Attorney: Consulting with an experienced intellectual property attorney is highly recommended to protect your intellectual assets effectively. An attorney can assist in conducting searches, preparing trademark applications or copyright registrations, and providing legal advice tailored to your specific needs. They can guide you through the process, help enforce your rights, and address any infringement issues that may arise.

5. Monitor and Enforce Your Rights: After obtaining trademark registrations or copyright protection, it is crucial to actively monitor and enforce your intellectual property rights. Regularly

monitor the market for potential infringements, and take appropriate legal action to protect your rights if unauthorized use is discovered. This may involve sending cease-and-desist letters, pursuing litigation, or negotiating licensing agreements.

6. International Protection: If you plan to expand your business internationally, consider obtaining intellectual property protection in other countries. This may involve filing trademark applications or copyright registrations with foreign intellectual property offices or leveraging international agreements and treaties for protection.

Remember that intellectual property laws can be complex, and proper legal guidance is essential to navigate the registration process and enforce your rights effectively. By protecting your intellectual assets, you safeguard your brand reputation, maintain a competitive edge, and maximize the value of your business.

Consulting with an intellectual property attorney is highly recommended to assess your specific intellectual property needs, develop a comprehensive strategy, and ensure that your intellectual assets are adequately protected.

Understanding insurance requirements:

Securing appropriate business insurance coverage is crucial to protect your assets and mitigate risks. In Florida, specific insurance requirements may apply based on your industry and business activities. Here are key considerations when obtaining business insurance:

1. General Liability Insurance: General liability insurance provides coverage for third-party claims related to bodily injury, property damage, or personal injury caused by your business operations. It safeguards your business from potential lawsuits and can cover legal defense costs, settlement amounts, or judgments. General liability insurance is typically essential for businesses of all types and sizes.

2. Professional Liability Insurance: Professional liability insurance, also known as errors and omissions insurance, is relevant for businesses that provide professional services or advice. It protects against claims of negligence, errors, or omissions that may arise from professional services rendered. Professional liability insurance provides coverage for legal defense costs and damages resulting from alleged professional negligence.

3. Workers' Compensation Insurance: Florida law requires most employers to carry workers' compensation insurance, which provides benefits to employees who suffer work-related injuries or illnesses. Workers' compensation insurance covers medical expenses, disability benefits, and lost wages for injured employees. Compliance with workers' compensation requirements is essential to protect your employees and comply with state regulations.

4. Property Insurance: Property insurance protects your physical assets, such as buildings, equipment, inventory, and fixtures, against damage or loss due to covered perils, such as fire, theft, or vandalism. It can also include business interruption coverage, which helps compensate for lost income and ongoing expenses if your business is temporarily unable to operate due to a covered event.

5. Business Interruption Insurance: Business interruption insurance provides coverage for lost income and ongoing expenses if your business operations are interrupted or suspended due to a covered event, such as a fire, natural disaster, or other unforeseen circumstances. It helps ensure financial stability during the recovery period.

6. Industry-Specific Insurance: Depending on your industry and business activities, additional insurance coverage may be necessary. For example, businesses in the healthcare industry may require medical malpractice insurance, while construction companies may need contractor's liability insurance. Assess your specific industry risks and consult with an insurance professional to determine the appropriate coverage for your business.

7. Insurance Requirements and Compliance: Research and understand any industry-specific insurance requirements imposed by regulatory bodies or contractual obligations. Certain professions or industries may have specific insurance mandates, such as minimum coverage limits or types of policies. Ensuring compliance with these requirements is essential to operate legally and protect your business interests.

Consulting with an insurance professional or broker specializing in commercial insurance can provide valuable guidance in selecting the right insurance policies tailored to your business's needs. They can help assess your risks, recommend appropriate coverage, and ensure compliance with Florida insurance regulations.

Remember, adequate business insurance coverage is a critical investment that safeguards your assets, mitigates risks, and provides peace of mind. Assess your insurance needs regularly as your business evolves and consult with professionals to ensure you have comprehensive coverage for your specific industry and operational risks.

Establishing a professional network of advisors:

Building a network of trusted advisors is indeed essential for the success of your business. Here are key professionals to consider engaging as part of your advisory team:

1. Business Attorney: A business attorney with expertise in Florida business law can provide valuable guidance on legal compliance, contract drafting and negotiation, intellectual property protection, employment matters, and other legal issues specific to your business. They can help you navigate legal complexities, ensure compliance with regulations, and protect your business interests.

2. Accountant or CPA: An accountant or certified public accountant (CPA) can assist with financial management, bookkeeping, tax planning, and compliance with tax obligations. They can provide valuable insights on tax strategies, financial statements, cash flow management, and ensure that your financial records are accurate and in compliance with accounting standards and regulations.

3. Business Consultant: A business consultant can provide expertise in various areas, such as market analysis, strategic planning, operations optimization, and business development. They can offer an objective perspective, help identify opportunities for growth, and guide you in making informed decisions to enhance your business performance.

4. Insurance Professional: An insurance professional or broker specializing in commercial insurance can help you assess your business's insurance needs and identify appropriate coverage to mitigate risks. They can guide you in selecting the right policies, ensure compliance with insurance requirements, and provide ongoing support as your business evolves.

5. Financial Advisor: A financial advisor can assist in developing financial strategies, investment planning, retirement planning, and risk management. They can help you make informed decisions about capital allocation, funding options, and long-term financial goals to ensure the financial health and sustainability of your business.

6. Industry Associations and Business Organizations: Engaging with industry associations and business organizations relevant to your field can provide networking opportunities, industry insights, and access to resources and educational events. These organizations often offer valuable resources, mentorship programs, and connections that can support your business growth.

When selecting advisors, seek professionals with relevant experience and expertise in the specific needs of your industry and business stage. Conduct interviews, ask for referrals, and assess their track record before establishing long-term partnerships.

Remember, communication and collaboration with your advisory team are crucial. Regularly consult with them to discuss challenges, seek guidance, and ensure that your business strategies align with legal requirements, financial objectives, and industry best practices.

By building a network of trusted advisors, you leverage the expertise and knowledge of professionals who can provide valuable guidance, support decision-making, and help navigate the complex landscape of starting and operating a business in Florida. Their insights and assistance can contribute significantly to your business's success and long-term growth.

By diligently completing these registration steps, you lay the foundation for a legally compliant and well-structured business in Florida. Remember, compliance with state and local regulations is crucial to avoid legal issues and maintain a favorable operating environment. Seek professional assistance as needed to navigate the complexities of business registration and ensure a solid start for your venture in the Sunshine State.

Chapter 3:

Managing Finances and Accounting

Effectively managing finances and maintaining accurate accounting records are crucial for the success and stability of your small business in Florida. This chapter provides guidance on key financial aspects and best practices to help you maintain control and make informed financial decisions.

Setting up a business bank account:

Establishing a separate business bank account is a critical step in managing your business's finances effectively. Here are important considerations when opening a business bank account:

1. Choose a Reputable Bank: Select a reputable bank that offers business banking services tailored to your needs. Research various financial institutions, compare account features, fees, and customer reviews to find the best fit for your business.
2. Business Entity Documentation: Prepare the necessary documentation to open a business bank account. This typically includes your business formation documents (e.g., Articles of Incorporation, Certificate of Formation), Employer Identification Number (EIN) from the IRS, and any other relevant legal documentation specific to your business structure.
3. Determine the Account Type: Depending on your business structure, you may choose from different account types, such as a business checking account, savings account, or merchant account for online transactions. Consider your business's cash flow, transaction volume, and financial goals to determine the most suitable account type.
4. Business Name and Legal Entity: Ensure that the account is opened in your business's legal name. This reinforces the separation between personal and business finances, provides a professional image, and simplifies record-keeping for tax and accounting purposes.
5. Keep Personal and Business Finances Separate: Maintaining separate accounts for personal and business finances is crucial. Avoid mixing personal and business expenses or using your business account for personal transactions. This separation improves financial clarity, streamlines accounting processes, and helps protect personal assets.

6. Access and Online Banking Services: Evaluate the bank's accessibility, including branch locations, ATM availability, and online banking services. Online banking platforms provide convenience, allowing you to manage your accounts, monitor transactions, and make electronic payments securely.
7. Obtain Business Debit or Credit Cards: Consider obtaining a business debit card or credit card linked to your business account. These cards can simplify expense tracking, facilitate cash flow management, and provide a dedicated payment method for business-related transactions.
8. Explore Additional Services: Inquire about additional services that may benefit your business, such as merchant services for accepting credit card payments, payroll services, or business loans. Assess your current and future financial needs to determine the most suitable banking services for your business.
9. Maintain Accurate Records: Ensure proper record-keeping by documenting all financial transactions related to your business. Keep track of deposits, expenses, invoices, and receipts. This practice simplifies accounting, tax reporting, and financial analysis, ensuring compliance with legal and regulatory requirements.

Opening a separate business bank account establishes a clear distinction between personal and business finances, enhances financial transparency, and demonstrates professionalism to clients, vendors, and financial institutions. It also simplifies financial management, tax reporting, and compliance with legal and regulatory obligations.

Consult with a business attorney or accountant to ensure you meet all legal and financial requirements when opening a business bank account. They can provide guidance tailored to your specific business structure and industry, helping you make informed decisions that support the financial health and success of your business.

Implementing bookkeeping and accounting systems:

Implementing a robust bookkeeping system is indeed crucial for maintaining accurate and organized financial records. Here are key steps to consider:

1. Choose Accounting Software: Select accounting software that suits the needs and size of your business. Popular options include QuickBooks, Xero, and FreshBooks. These platforms

provide features such as income and expense tracking, invoicing, financial reporting, and integration with banking accounts.

2. Set Up Chart of Accounts: Develop a chart of accounts, which categorizes income, expenses, assets, liabilities, and equity. This structure organizes financial transactions and facilitates accurate tracking and reporting.

3. Record Income and Expenses: Regularly record all business income and expenses in your bookkeeping system. Capture details such as dates, amounts, payees, and descriptions. Assign appropriate account categories to each transaction.

4. Manage Accounts Receivable and Accounts Payable: Track and monitor outstanding customer invoices (accounts receivable) and amounts owed to vendors (accounts payable). This ensures timely collections and payments, supporting healthy cash flow management.

5. Reconcile Bank Statements: Regularly reconcile your bank and credit card statements with your bookkeeping records. This process ensures accuracy and identifies any discrepancies that require attention.

6. Generate Financial Reports: Utilize your accounting software to generate essential financial reports, such as profit and loss statements, balance sheets, and cash flow statements. These reports provide insights into your business's financial performance, helping you make informed decisions.

7. Maintain Documented Records: Retain copies of invoices, receipts, and other supporting documents for each financial transaction. These records are essential for tax purposes, audits, and financial analysis.

8. Engage a Professional Bookkeeper: If managing your bookkeeping becomes overwhelming, consider engaging a professional bookkeeper. They can assist with setting up your bookkeeping system, ensuring accurate data entry, and providing ongoing support to maintain your financial records.

9. Regularly Review and Analyze Financial Data: Take time to review and analyze your financial data regularly. Assess your business's financial health, identify trends, and make informed decisions based on the insights gained from your bookkeeping records.

Maintaining a robust bookkeeping system not only enables accurate financial reporting but also provides a clear understanding of your business's financial position. It supports tax compliance, aids in budgeting and financial planning, and helps demonstrate financial stability to investors, lenders, or potential partners.

If you lack bookkeeping expertise, consider consulting with an accountant or bookkeeping professional who can guide you in setting up and maintaining an effective bookkeeping system. Their expertise ensures adherence to accounting principles and regulatory requirements, providing you with peace of mind and accurate financial information for your business.

Understanding financial statements and reports:

Familiarizing yourself with basic financial statements is indeed essential for understanding and evaluating your business's financial performance. Here's an overview of the three primary financial statements:

1. Income Statement (Profit and Loss Statement): The income statement summarizes your business's revenues, expenses, and net income or loss over a specific period. It provides a snapshot of your profitability by showing how much revenue you generated and the costs incurred to generate that revenue. By analyzing the income statement, you can assess your business's ability to generate profits.

2. Balance Sheet: The balance sheet provides a snapshot of your business's financial position at a specific point in time. It presents your assets, liabilities, and equity. Assets include cash, accounts receivable, inventory, and property. Liabilities include accounts payable, loans, and other obligations. Equity represents the residual interest in the business after deducting liabilities from assets. The balance sheet helps assess your business's solvency and financial health.

3. Cash Flow Statement: The cash flow statement tracks the flow of cash into and out of your business during a specific period. It categorizes cash flows into operating activities (e.g., revenue, expenses), investing activities (e.g., purchases or sales of assets), and financing activities (e.g., loans, equity investments). The cash flow statement provides insights into your business's liquidity and ability to generate and manage cash.

Regularly reviewing and analyzing these financial statements is crucial for financial management and decision-making. Here are key considerations:

1. Assess Profitability: Examine your income statement to understand your business's revenue sources, cost of goods sold, operating expenses, and net income. Compare your revenues and expenses over time to identify trends and evaluate profitability.

2. Evaluate Financial Position: Analyze your balance sheet to assess the value of your assets, obligations, and equity. Calculate financial ratios such as liquidity ratios (e.g., current ratio), leverage ratios (e.g., debt-to-equity ratio), and profitability ratios (e.g., return on assets) to evaluate your business's financial health.

3. Monitor Cash Flow: The cash flow statement helps you track the cash inflows and outflows of your business. Evaluate the operating, investing, and financing activities to understand the sources and uses of cash. Identify any cash flow challenges or opportunities for improvement.

4. Make Informed Decisions: By regularly reviewing and analyzing these financial statements, you can make informed decisions regarding pricing, cost control, investments, financing, and overall business strategies. Identify areas of strength and weakness to optimize your financial performance.

If you are unfamiliar with financial statements or require assistance in their interpretation, consider consulting with an accountant or financial advisor. They can guide you through the analysis process, provide insights into your business's financial health, and help you make informed decisions to drive your business's success.

Remember, understanding and analyzing financial statements is an ongoing process. Regularly review and update these statements to stay informed about your business's financial performance and make proactive adjustments as needed.

Managing cash flow and budgeting:

Cash flow management is indeed a critical aspect of running a small business. Developing a cash flow budget and implementing effective strategies can help ensure adequate liquidity and financial stability. Here are key steps to consider:

1. Forecast Cash Flow: Create a cash flow budget by estimating your expected cash inflows and outflows over a specific period, such as monthly or quarterly. Include revenue projections, accounts receivable collections, operating expenses, accounts payable payments, loan repayments, and other cash transactions.
2. Monitor Cash Flow Regularly: Review your actual cash inflows and outflows against your budgeted projections on a regular basis. This allows you to identify any discrepancies, potential cash flow issues, or areas of improvement. Regular monitoring enables proactive decision-making and helps maintain financial stability.
3. Optimize Accounts Receivable: Implement effective accounts receivable management strategies to minimize late payments and improve cash flow. Set clear payment terms, send timely and accurate invoices, follow up on overdue payments, and consider offering incentives for early payments.
4. Manage Accounts Payable: Manage your accounts payable strategically to optimize cash flow. Negotiate favorable payment terms with suppliers, take advantage of early payment discounts if available, and ensure timely payment to avoid late fees or penalties.
5. Control Expenses: Review your operating expenses regularly to identify areas where costs can be reduced without compromising the quality of your products or services. Consider renegotiating contracts with vendors, finding more cost-effective alternatives, and closely monitoring discretionary spending.
6. Plan for Capital Expenditures: Anticipate and plan for any significant capital expenditures or investments in your cash flow budget. This allows you to allocate funds and plan financing options in advance, reducing the impact on your cash flow.
7. Explore Financing Options: In cases of temporary cash flow shortages, explore financing options such as a line of credit, short-term loans, or invoice financing to bridge the gap. Carefully consider the costs and terms associated with these options and assess their impact on your cash flow.
8. Maintain a Cash Reserve: Establish and maintain a cash reserve or contingency fund to cover unexpected expenses or emergencies. This provides a cushion to help manage cash flow fluctuations and avoid financial strain.

9. Seek Professional Advice: Consider consulting with an accountant or financial advisor who specializes in small business cash flow management. They can provide guidance tailored to your specific circumstances, offer insights into best practices, and help you optimize your cash flow management strategies.

By developing a cash flow budget, monitoring your cash flow regularly, and implementing effective strategies, you can maintain a healthy cash position and navigate potential cash flow challenges. Effective cash flow management is essential for sustaining and growing your business in the long term.

Tracking expenses and managing receipts:

Maintaining detailed and organized records of your business expenses is essential for proper financial management, tax compliance, and accurate reporting. Here are key steps to consider:

1. Capture and Organize Receipts: Keep a record of all business-related receipts, invoices, and documentation. Store them in a designated location, either physically or digitally, for easy retrieval and reference. Consider using expense management software or apps to digitize and categorize receipts for streamlined record-keeping.
2. Categorize Expenses: Categorize your expenses based on common expense categories such as supplies, rent, utilities, marketing, professional services, and travel. This categorization helps organize your expenses and simplifies tracking and reporting for tax purposes.
3. Maintain an Expense Log: Keep a comprehensive expense log or ledger to record each expense, including the date, description, amount, and category. Include any relevant details, such as the purpose of the expense or the client/customer associated with it. This log serves as a central record of all your business expenses.
4. Reconcile Bank and Credit Card Statements: Regularly reconcile your bank and credit card statements with your expense records. This process ensures accuracy and helps identify any discrepancies or missing transactions.
5. Separate Personal and Business Expenses: Maintain clear separation between personal and business expenses. Use separate bank accounts and credit cards for your business

transactions to avoid commingling funds. This separation simplifies record-keeping and helps demonstrate the legitimacy of business expenses.

6. Implement Accounting Software: Consider using accounting software to streamline expense management, automate categorization, and generate accurate financial reports. Many software options are available, ranging from basic to advanced features, depending on your business needs.

7. Stay Updated on Tax Regulations: Familiarize yourself with tax regulations applicable to your business and ensure compliance with reporting requirements. Keep track of any deductible expenses, such as business-related travel, meals, or home office expenses, to maximize your tax deductions.

8. Consult with an Accountant: Engaging an accountant or tax professional can provide valuable guidance and ensure accurate financial record-keeping and tax compliance. They can help you navigate complex tax laws, identify eligible deductions, and ensure your financial records align with legal requirements.

By maintaining detailed records, categorizing expenses, and staying organized, you establish a strong foundation for financial management and reporting. Accurate record-keeping not only simplifies tax preparation but also provides valuable insights into your business's financial health and performance.

Implementing effective inventory management:

Efficient inventory management is indeed vital for businesses that involve selling products. Inventory management encompasses various processes and systems that help track and control the flow of goods in and out of your business. By implementing effective inventory management practices, you can optimize stock levels, reduce carrying costs, and ensure that you have the right products available to meet customer demand.

One key aspect of inventory management is tracking inventory levels accurately. This involves regularly monitoring the quantity of each product in stock and updating the records accordingly. Utilizing inventory management software can streamline this process by automating the tracking and reporting of inventory levels. Such software can provide real-time visibility into stock quantities, enable automatic reordering based on predetermined thresholds, and generate reports for analysis and decision-making.

Determining reorder points is another critical aspect of inventory management. By setting appropriate reorder points, you can ensure that you replenish inventory before it runs out. This requires forecasting demand, considering lead times for restocking, and accounting for any seasonal or promotional variations in sales. Setting optimal reorder points helps prevent stockouts and ensures that you can fulfill customer orders in a timely manner.

Managing stock turnover is an essential consideration for inventory management. Stock turnover refers to how quickly you sell and replace your inventory. By monitoring and analyzing stock turnover ratios, you can identify slow-moving or obsolete inventory and take appropriate actions, such as adjusting pricing, implementing promotions, or discontinuing certain products. Maximizing stock turnover helps improve cash flow, reduces carrying costs, and ensures that your inventory remains fresh and relevant.

Efficient inventory management involves finding the right balance between carrying enough inventory to meet customer demand and avoiding excessive stock that ties up capital and storage space. Regularly conducting physical inventory counts, reconciling them with your records, and addressing any discrepancies is crucial for maintaining accurate inventory levels.

Ultimately, implementing effective inventory management practices contributes to improved customer satisfaction, streamlined operations, and better financial performance. Whether through the utilization of inventory management software or manual tracking methods, it is essential to establish systems that align with your business's specific needs and ensure efficient inventory control.

By adopting efficient inventory management practices, you can enhance your business's overall profitability, minimize stock-related issues, and deliver a seamless customer experience by having the right products available at the right time.

Establishing pricing strategies and profit margins:

Determining the appropriate pricing strategies for your products or services is a crucial aspect of running a successful business. Pricing decisions impact your revenue, profitability, market positioning, and customer perception. To establish effective pricing strategies, it is important to consider various factors and conduct thorough analysis.

Firstly, understanding your cost structure is essential. Calculate your direct costs, including the cost of materials, labor, and any other expenses directly related to producing your products or delivering your services. Additionally, consider indirect costs such as overhead expenses, marketing costs, and administrative expenses. Knowing your costs enables you to set pricing that covers expenses and allows for a reasonable profit margin.

Market demand and customer preferences also play a significant role in pricing decisions. Conduct market research to understand how customers perceive the value of your products or services and what they are willing to pay. Assess your target market's purchasing power, price sensitivity, and their expectations regarding quality and features. This information helps you align your pricing with customer expectations and capture the perceived value of your offerings.

Analyzing the competition is another critical step in establishing pricing strategies. Evaluate the pricing models and strategies of your competitors, considering factors such as their market position, product differentiation, and target audience. Determine whether you want to position your business as a low-cost provider, a premium brand, or somewhere in between. This analysis helps you understand how your pricing compares to the market and identify opportunities for differentiation or price optimization.

Profitability goals should also guide your pricing decisions. Determine your desired profit margins and assess whether your pricing strategies align with those goals. Take into account factors such as sales volume, economies of scale, and the pricing elasticity of your products or services. Regularly review and analyze your pricing structure to ensure that it supports your profitability objectives.

It is important to note that pricing is not a one-time decision. It should be an ongoing process that is regularly reviewed and adjusted based on market dynamics, cost fluctuations, and competitive factors. Monitor customer feedback, track sales performance, and conduct periodic pricing analyses to assess the effectiveness of your pricing strategies.

Communication is key when implementing pricing changes. Clearly communicate any price adjustments to your customers, explaining the value proposition and benefits associated with your offerings. Consider offering promotional discounts, loyalty programs, or bundling options to incentivize customer purchases.

By considering your costs, market demand, competition, and desired profit margins, you can establish pricing strategies that optimize profitability while remaining competitive in the market. Regularly reviewing and adjusting your pricing strategies ensures that your business remains responsive to market conditions and continues to deliver value to customers while achieving your financial objectives.

Complying with tax obligations and record-keeping:

As a Florida business owner, it is important to understand and fulfill your tax obligations to maintain compliance with state and federal tax laws. By staying informed about the tax requirements and implementing effective financial management practices, you can ensure accurate reporting, minimize the risk of penalties or audits, and optimize your business's financial health.

One of the primary tax obligations for Florida businesses is sales tax. If your business sells taxable goods or services, you are generally required to collect and remit sales tax to the Florida Department of Revenue. Familiarize yourself with the specific sales tax rates and exemptions applicable to your industry and products. Establish systems to accurately track and report sales tax collections and maintain proper records to support your sales tax filings.

Payroll taxes are another important consideration for businesses with employees. You must withhold federal income tax, Social Security tax, and Medicare tax from your employees' wages and remit those amounts to the appropriate government agencies. Additionally, you are responsible for paying the employer's portion of Social Security and Medicare taxes. Ensure that you understand the federal and state payroll tax requirements, including filing deadlines, reporting obligations, and the proper calculation of tax withholdings.

Federal income taxes also apply to businesses in Florida. Depending on your business structure, you may be subject to different tax rules. For example, sole proprietors report business income and expenses on their personal tax returns, while corporations are subject to separate tax filings. Consult with a tax professional or accountant to determine the appropriate federal income tax requirements for your business and ensure accurate reporting and compliance.

Maintaining organized financial records is crucial for tax compliance and financial management. Keep detailed records of all business transactions, including sales, expenses, payroll records, and supporting documentation such as receipts and invoices. These records serve as evidence to support your tax filings and can help you respond to any inquiries or audits from tax authorities.

Regularly review and stay updated on changes to tax laws and regulations. Tax laws can evolve, and it is important to stay informed about any updates that may impact your business's tax obligations. Consider engaging with accounting professionals or tax advisors who can provide guidance and ensure that you are aware of any changes and taking advantage of available tax benefits or incentives.

By implementing effective financial management practices, including accurate record-keeping, understanding tax obligations, and seeking professional advice when needed, you can maintain compliance with tax laws, optimize your tax planning strategies, and establish a solid financial foundation for your Florida business. Remember, proactive tax management not only helps you meet your obligations but also provides opportunities to minimize tax liabilities and maximize your business's financial success.

Chapter 4:

Employment and Labor Law

Understanding and complying with employment and labor laws is crucial when hiring and managing employees for your small business in Florida. This chapter provides an overview of key considerations to ensure legal compliance and foster a positive and productive work environment.

Understanding employment classifications (employee vs. independent contractor):

Properly classifying workers as either employees or independent contractors is crucial to ensure compliance with employment and tax laws. While the distinction between the two can sometimes be complex, understanding the criteria established by federal and state laws will help you make accurate determinations.

The Internal Revenue Service (IRS) provides guidelines to assess worker classification for federal tax purposes. These guidelines focus on three main categories: behavioral control, financial control, and the nature of the relationship between the worker and the business. Factors such as the degree of control the business exercises over the worker's activities, the method of payment, the provision of benefits, and the permanency of the relationship are considered in this assessment.

The Florida Department of Revenue also provides guidance on worker classification for state tax purposes. In Florida, the common law test is applied to determine the employer-employee relationship. Factors such as the employer's right to control the details of the work, the provision of tools and equipment, the payment method, and the degree of skill required are considered in this assessment.

It is important to note that worker classification can have significant implications for both the employer and the worker. Misclassifying workers can result in legal consequences, such as back taxes, penalties, and potential liability for unpaid wages or benefits. Additionally, misclassification can affect workers' eligibility for certain benefits and protections, such as minimum wage, overtime pay, workers' compensation, and unemployment insurance.

To properly classify workers, thoroughly evaluate the nature of the relationship and assess the factors outlined by the IRS and the Florida Department of Revenue. If you are uncertain about worker classification, consult with an employment law attorney or seek professional advice to ensure compliance with the applicable laws and regulations.

Remember, accurate worker classification is essential for maintaining legal compliance, protecting your business from potential liabilities, and ensuring fair treatment of workers. Stay informed about changes in employment laws and seek professional guidance to navigate the complexities of worker classification in your Florida business.

Complying with federal and state employment laws:

Understanding federal and state labor laws is crucial for small businesses in Florida to ensure compliance and promote fair and equitable employment practices. Familiarize yourself with key federal laws, such as the Fair Labor Standards Act (FLSA), which sets standards for minimum wage, overtime pay, and child labor, and the Family and Medical Leave Act (FMLA), which provides eligible employees with job-protected leave for certain medical and family reasons.

Additionally, be aware of the Americans with Disabilities Act (ADA), which prohibits discrimination against individuals with disabilities and requires reasonable accommodations in the workplace. Compliance with the ADA ensures equal employment opportunities and accessibility for qualified individuals.

In Florida, specific labor laws and regulations also apply. For example, the Florida Minimum Wage Act establishes minimum wage requirements that may differ from the federal minimum wage. It is important to stay informed about any changes in minimum wage rates and adjust your payroll practices accordingly.

The Florida Civil Rights Act prohibits discrimination in employment based on various protected characteristics, including race, color, religion, sex, national origin, age, and disability. Compliance with these anti-discrimination laws is essential to maintain a diverse and inclusive work environment.

To ensure compliance with labor laws, regularly review and update your employment policies and practices. Develop an employee handbook that clearly outlines company policies, procedures, and expectations. Provide training to managers and supervisors on equal employment opportunity, harassment prevention, and ADA compliance.

Seeking legal counsel or consulting with an employment law attorney can provide valuable guidance tailored to your specific business needs. They can help you understand and navigate the complex landscape of labor laws, ensuring that your business maintains compliance and fosters a positive work environment.

Remember, compliance with federal and state labor laws is not only a legal obligation but also contributes to a fair and respectful workplace. By prioritizing compliance and promoting a culture of inclusivity and equal opportunity, you enhance your business's reputation, attract and retain talented employees, and minimize the risk of costly legal disputes..

Hiring and onboarding employees:

Developing effective hiring practices is crucial for small businesses in Florida to attract and retain top talent while ensuring compliance with legal requirements. Adhering to fair and non-discriminatory practices promotes equal employment opportunities and helps build a diverse and inclusive workforce.

To establish a standardized hiring process, begin by clearly defining the job requirements, qualifications, and responsibilities. Develop job postings that accurately reflect the position and comply with relevant employment laws, such as the Equal Employment Opportunity Commission (EEOC) guidelines. Advertise job openings through appropriate channels, such as online job boards, industry-specific platforms, or local career fairs.

Conduct interviews in a structured and consistent manner, focusing on the candidate's qualifications and fit for the position. Ensure that interview questions comply with anti-discrimination laws and do not inquire about protected characteristics, such as age, race, religion, or disability. Instead, focus on evaluating the candidate's skills, experience, and ability to perform the job.

Perform background checks on potential employees, keeping in mind that certain restrictions and guidelines apply to background checks, such as compliance with the Fair Credit Reporting Act (FCRA). Seek legal advice or consult with a background screening service to ensure compliance with relevant laws and regulations.

Once you have selected a candidate, properly onboard them into your organization. Provide necessary training, orientation, and information about company policies and procedures. Comply with employment eligibility verification requirements by completing and retaining Form I-9 for each new employee, ensuring they are authorized to work in the United States.

It is important to stay informed about changes in employment laws and regulations. Regularly review and update your hiring practices, employee handbooks, and policies to ensure compliance with evolving legal requirements. Seek guidance from employment law attorneys or human resources professionals to address any specific concerns or legal complexities related to your industry or business.

By implementing fair and compliant hiring practices, you demonstrate your commitment to equal opportunity, attract qualified candidates, and reduce the risk of potential legal disputes. Hiring and onboarding processes that emphasize fairness and legality contribute to a positive employer brand, fostering a productive and engaged workforce.

Developing employment contracts and agreements:

Using written employment contracts is a prudent practice for small businesses in Florida to establish clear expectations and protect the rights and interests of both the employer and the employee. Employment contracts provide a legally binding agreement that outlines the terms and conditions of employment, ensuring a mutual understanding of rights, obligations, and expectations.

When drafting an employment contract, it is crucial to include key elements such as:

1. Terms of Employment: Clearly define the nature of the employment relationship, including the position, start date, work schedule, and duration of employment (if applicable).
2. Compensation and Benefits: Specify the employee's salary, bonuses, commission structures (if applicable), and any additional benefits, such as health insurance, retirement plans, or vacation and sick leave policies.
3. Confidentiality and Intellectual Property Rights: Protect your business's proprietary information by including provisions that require employees to maintain confidentiality and not disclose or use confidential information during or after employment. Address intellectual property rights, ensuring that any work created by the employee during their employment is owned by the business.

4. Non-Compete and Non-Solicitation Agreements: Depending on the nature of your business, you may consider including non-compete and non-solicitation clauses to restrict employees from engaging in competitive activities or soliciting clients or employees for a certain period after their employment ends. Note that non-compete agreements in Florida are subject to specific legal requirements and restrictions.

5. Dispute Resolution Mechanisms: Include provisions for resolving employment-related disputes, such as arbitration or mediation clauses, which can provide a faster and more cost-effective alternative to litigation.

It is essential to consult with an employment attorney to ensure that your employment contracts comply with federal and state employment laws, as well as any industry-specific regulations. An attorney can help tailor the contracts to your business's unique needs and objectives, provide guidance on legal requirements, and ensure that the agreements are enforceable under Florida law.

Regularly review and update employment contracts as needed to reflect changes in employment laws, business practices, or the specific needs of your organization. Seeking legal counsel and periodically revisiting employment contracts demonstrate your commitment to fair employment practices and mitigate the risk of potential disputes or legal challenges.

Remember, employment contracts serve as a valuable tool for clarifying expectations, protecting business interests, and fostering a positive and professional employment relationship. By utilizing written employment contracts, you establish a solid foundation for your business's employment practices and mitigate potential legal risks.

Managing employee benefits and compensation:

Compliance with federal and state laws regarding employee benefits and compensation is essential for small businesses in Florida. Adhering to these regulations ensures fair treatment of employees, maintains legal compliance, and helps establish a positive and productive work environment. Here are some key considerations:

1. Minimum Wage: Familiarize yourself with both the federal and Florida state minimum wage requirements. Ensure that all employees receive at least the applicable minimum wage for the hours they work.

2. Overtime Pay: Understand the criteria for determining eligibility for overtime pay as per the Fair Labor Standards Act (FLSA). Non-exempt employees who work more than 40 hours in a workweek are generally entitled to overtime pay at a rate of one and a half times their regular hourly wage.
3. Meal and Rest Breaks: Know the requirements for providing meal and rest breaks to employees. While federal law does not mandate these breaks, Florida law has specific provisions for breaks in certain industries, such as minors and nursing mothers.
4. Affordable Care Act (ACA): If your business meets the criteria for offering health insurance coverage under the ACA, ensure compliance with the requirements, such as providing affordable coverage and submitting necessary reporting forms.
5. Workers' Compensation: In Florida, most employers are required to carry workers' compensation insurance. This coverage protects employees in the event of work-related injuries or illnesses and provides them with medical benefits and wage replacement.
6. Unemployment Insurance: Register with the Florida Department of Economic Opportunity to fulfill your obligations for unemployment insurance. This program provides temporary financial assistance to employees who become unemployed through no fault of their own.
7. Other Statutory Benefits: Familiarize yourself with additional benefits mandated by federal or state laws, such as family and medical leave, pregnancy accommodations, and disability accommodations.

Implementing a fair and consistent compensation structure is also crucial. Establish clear and transparent policies for determining employee compensation, considering factors such as job responsibilities, experience, performance, and market rates. It is essential to ensure that compensation practices do not discriminate based on protected characteristics, such as race, gender, age, or disability.

Regularly review and update your policies and practices to remain in compliance with changing laws and regulations. Consult with an employment attorney or human resources professional who can provide guidance specific to your business and industry.

Remember, prioritizing compliance with employee benefits and compensation laws is not only a legal requirement but also a reflection of your commitment to fair and ethical employment practices. It helps build trust with your employees, contributes to a positive work environment, and mitigates the risk of legal disputes and penalties.

Implementing workplace safety and health measures:

Ensuring employee safety is a paramount responsibility for small businesses in Florida. Compliance with the Occupational Safety and Health Act (OSHA) regulations is vital to providing a safe work environment and protecting the well-being of your employees. Here are some key considerations:

1. Risk Assessment: Conduct a thorough assessment of your workplace to identify potential hazards and risks. This may involve evaluating machinery, equipment, chemicals, and other elements that could pose a threat to employee safety.
2. Safety Policies and Procedures: Establish comprehensive safety policies and procedures that address identified hazards and outline guidelines for safe work practices. Communicate these policies to all employees and provide appropriate training to ensure their understanding and compliance.
3. Training and Education: Provide regular safety training to employees, emphasizing proper handling of equipment, adherence to safety protocols, and awareness of potential hazards. This training should be ongoing and include updates on new safety regulations or procedures.
4. Hazard Communication: Comply with OSHA's Hazard Communication Standard (HazCom) by properly labeling hazardous substances, providing Safety Data Sheets (SDS) for chemicals, and ensuring employees have access to necessary information regarding potential workplace hazards.
5. Personal Protective Equipment (PPE): Assess the need for personal protective equipment based on the nature of your business and the identified hazards. Provide appropriate PPE to employees and ensure they are trained on its correct usage and maintenance.
6. Reporting and Investigation: Establish a process for reporting and investigating workplace accidents, injuries, near misses, or safety concerns. Promptly address any identified issues and implement corrective actions to prevent future incidents.

7. OSHA Compliance: Stay informed about OSHA regulations applicable to your industry and ensure compliance with all requirements. Regularly review and update your safety programs to align with any changes in regulations.
8. Recordkeeping: Maintain accurate records of safety training, incident reports, safety inspections, and any other relevant safety documentation as required by OSHA.

It is essential to create a culture of safety within your organization, where employees feel empowered to report safety concerns and participate actively in maintaining a safe work environment. Encourage open communication, provide avenues for feedback, and recognize and reward employees for their commitment to safety.

Consult with safety experts, attend OSHA training programs, and consider engaging the services of safety consultants or professionals with expertise in your industry. Their guidance can help ensure that your business meets or exceeds safety standards, reducing the risk of workplace accidents, injuries, and potential legal liabilities.

Remember, prioritizing employee safety not only protects your employees but also enhances productivity, morale, and the overall reputation of your business. By investing in safety measures and compliance, you create a work environment that fosters well-being and contributes to the long-term success of your business.

Preventing discrimination and harassment in the workplace:

Creating a workplace environment that is free from discrimination and harassment is not only essential for legal compliance but also for fostering a positive and inclusive work culture. Here are key steps to consider:

1. Develop Anti-Discrimination and Harassment Policies: Establish clear policies that explicitly prohibit discrimination and harassment based on protected characteristics. These policies should outline expectations, reporting procedures, and consequences for violations. Ensure that these policies are communicated to all employees and readily accessible.
2. Educate Employees: Conduct regular training sessions to educate employees about their rights and responsibilities related to discrimination and harassment prevention. Provide examples of prohibited behaviors and guidance on appropriate workplace conduct. Training should also address bystander

intervention and encourage employees to report any incidents they witness or experience.

3. Implement Reporting Mechanisms: Create a confidential and accessible reporting system for employees to report incidents of discrimination or harassment. Ensure that employees are aware of the reporting procedures, including multiple avenues for reporting, such as a designated person or an anonymous hotline. Promptly investigate all reports and take appropriate action.

4. Prompt and Thorough Investigations: When a complaint is filed, promptly and thoroughly investigate the matter. Assign the investigation to an impartial individual or team trained in conducting investigations. Maintain confidentiality throughout the process, and ensure that all parties involved are treated fairly and respectfully.

5. Enforce Consequences: If an investigation substantiates a complaint, take appropriate disciplinary action against the perpetrator, which may include warnings, training, suspension, or termination. Make it clear that discrimination and harassment will not be tolerated in the workplace.

6. Foster a Culture of Respect and Inclusion: Encourage an inclusive work environment where diversity is celebrated and all employees are treated with respect. Promote teamwork, collaboration, and mutual respect through team-building exercises, diversity training, and ongoing communication. Lead by example, demonstrating inclusive behaviors and addressing any discriminatory or harassing conduct swiftly.

7. Regular Policy Review and Updates: Periodically review and update your anti-discrimination and harassment policies to align with changes in laws or best practices. Stay informed about federal and state regulations and ensure compliance with any new requirements. Communicate policy updates to employees and provide refresher training as necessary.

8. Seek Legal Counsel: Consult with an employment attorney experienced in discrimination and harassment laws to ensure that your policies and procedures are comprehensive, compliant, and tailored to your specific business needs.

By actively promoting a workplace culture of respect, inclusivity, and zero tolerance for discrimination and harassment, you create an environment where employees can thrive and contribute to the success of your business. Committing to these principles not only ensures legal compliance but also enhances employee morale, engagement, and productivity.

Terminating employees and handling employment disputes:

When it comes to terminating employees, it is crucial to navigate the process carefully to ensure compliance with applicable laws and minimize the risk of legal disputes. Here are some important considerations and best practices:

1. Understand Employment Contracts and At-Will Employment: Review employment contracts, offer letters, or any other agreements that may specify the terms of employment and conditions for termination. Familiarize yourself with the concept of at-will employment, which allows employers to terminate employees for any reason that is not unlawful.
2. Adhere to Notice Requirements: Follow federal and state requirements regarding providing notice of termination to employees. Some states have specific notice periods depending on the length of employment or the number of employees affected. Ensure that termination notices are delivered in writing and include the effective date of termination.
3. Final Paychecks: Review federal and state laws regarding the timing and payment of final wages. Some states require employers to issue final paychecks immediately upon termination, while others may allow a reasonable period for payment. Calculate and provide all owed wages, including any accrued but unused vacation or paid time off (PTO) balances.
4. Compliance with Benefit Continuation: Determine the extent to which employee benefits, such as health insurance coverage, can be continued after termination. Understand the requirements under the Consolidated Omnibus Budget Reconciliation Act (COBRA) and state continuation coverage laws, if applicable. Provide employees with information on their rights and options for continued coverage.
5. Document Performance Issues and Termination Reasons: Maintain thorough and objective documentation of any performance issues or misconduct that led to the termination decision. Document warnings, coaching sessions, disciplinary actions, and any attempts made to address performance

concerns. This documentation can serve as evidence to support the termination decision if challenged.

6. Conduct Exit Interviews: Offer employees the opportunity to participate in exit interviews to provide feedback and discuss their experience with the company. These interviews can offer insights into areas for improvement and potentially help prevent future legal disputes.

7. Avoid Discrimination and Retaliation: Ensure that termination decisions are based on legitimate, non-discriminatory reasons, such as poor performance, misconduct, or business-related factors. Avoid terminating employees based on protected characteristics, such as race, gender, age, religion, or disability. Retaliation against employees for engaging in protected activities, such as reporting violations or participating in investigations, is also strictly prohibited.

8. Consider Mediation or Alternative Dispute Resolution: In the event of employment disputes, explore mediation or alternative dispute resolution (ADR) options as an alternative to litigation. Mediation can help resolve disputes more amicably and cost-effectively, while allowing for open dialogue and potential resolution between the parties involved.

9. Seek Legal Advice: Consult with an employment attorney to ensure compliance with applicable federal, state, and local laws. An attorney can provide guidance on termination procedures, review termination letters or severance agreements, and help mitigate the risk of potential legal disputes.

Remember, each termination situation is unique, and it is crucial to approach each case with sensitivity and adherence to legal requirements. By following best practices, maintaining clear documentation, and seeking legal guidance when needed, you can minimize risks and handle terminations in a fair and legally compliant manner.

By adhering to employment and labor laws, you can create a fair and legally compliant work environment while minimizing the risk of costly legal disputes. Engage with employment law attorneys or HR professionals to ensure ongoing compliance, stay updated on legal developments, and foster positive employee relations within your small business in Florida.

Chapter 5:

Contracts and Legal Agreements

Contracts form the foundation of business relationships and transactions. Understanding contract law and effectively managing contracts is essential for small businesses in Florida. This chapter provides guidance on key aspects of contracts and legal agreements.

Understanding the basics of contract law:

Contract law is the cornerstone of business transactions, providing a legal framework for parties to enter into agreements. By understanding the basics of contract law, business owners can navigate the complexities of drafting, negotiating, and enforcing contracts. Key concepts such as offer and acceptance, consideration, contractual capacity, and legal purpose form the foundation of any valid and enforceable contract.

The concept of offer and acceptance refers to the mutual agreement between parties to enter into a contract. An offer is a clear and definite proposal made by one party to another, and acceptance occurs when the other party agrees to the terms of the offer. For a contract to be formed, there must be a meeting of the minds between the parties.

Consideration is another crucial element of contract law. It refers to something of value that is exchanged between the parties, such as money, goods, or services. Consideration is necessary to support the enforceability of a contract and ensures that both parties receive something in return for their obligations.

Contractual capacity refers to the legal ability of parties to enter into a contract. Generally, individuals must have the legal capacity to understand the terms and implications of the contract, and they must not be under duress or undue influence. Minors, individuals with mental incapacity, and those under the influence of drugs or alcohol may lack contractual capacity.

Additionally, contracts must have a legal purpose to be enforceable. The purpose of the contract should not violate any laws or public policy. Contracts that involve illegal activities or violate ethical standards are considered void and unenforceable.

Understanding these basic principles of contract law empowers small business owners to enter into agreements with confidence. It allows them to protect their rights, ensure fair and equitable terms, and seek legal remedies in the event of a breach or dispute. Consulting with an attorney specializing in contract law can provide further guidance and expertise in navigating the complexities of contracts and legal agreements.

Drafting and negotiating contracts:

Creating well-drafted contracts is crucial for small businesses to protect their interests and avoid potential disputes or misunderstandings. It is essential to use clear and concise language to articulate the rights and obligations of all parties involved. By clearly defining the scope of the agreement, the responsibilities of each party, and any specific terms or conditions, you can minimize the risk of confusion or misinterpretation.

Negotiation plays a vital role in the contract creation process. It allows parties to discuss and refine the terms of the agreement to reach a mutually beneficial outcome. During negotiations, it is important to consider the needs and objectives of all parties involved and strive for a fair and equitable agreement. By engaging in open and transparent discussions, you can address any potential concerns or areas of disagreement and work towards a resolution that satisfies all parties.

Seeking the guidance of an attorney experienced in contract law can provide valuable assistance during the contract creation process. An attorney can review and assess the terms of the contract, ensure legal compliance, and offer guidance on best practices. Their expertise can help identify any potential pitfalls or areas of risk and provide valuable insights to protect your business's interests.

Remember, a well-drafted contract serves as a legal document that establishes the rights and obligations of all parties involved. It is a powerful tool that can provide protection, clarity, and enforceability. Taking the time to create comprehensive contracts can save your business from potential legal disputes and provide a solid foundation for successful business relationships.

Types of contracts essential for small businesses:

Contracts play a critical role in protecting the interests of small businesses across various aspects of their operations. Here are some types of contracts that are essential for different areas of your business:

1. Customer/Client Contracts: These agreements establish the terms and conditions of your products or services when

entering into a business relationship with customers or clients. They outline important details such as pricing, payment terms, delivery or performance obligations, and dispute resolution mechanisms.

2. Vendor/Supplier Agreements: These contracts formalize the relationship with your suppliers or vendors. They specify the goods or services to be provided, pricing, delivery terms, quality standards, warranties, and any additional terms or conditions. Clear agreements with vendors help ensure the timely and reliable supply of goods or services.

3. Lease Contracts: If you lease commercial space for your business, a lease contract is crucial. It outlines the terms, duration, rent, and responsibilities of both the landlord and tenant. Lease agreements address important considerations such as maintenance, repairs, insurance requirements, and termination clauses.

4. Employment Contracts: When hiring employees, employment contracts define the terms and conditions of employment. These contracts cover important aspects such as job responsibilities, compensation, benefits, working hours, leave policies, confidentiality, and non-compete provisions. Employment contracts help establish clear expectations and protect the rights of both the employer and the employee.

5. Confidentiality Agreements: Also known as non-disclosure agreements (NDAs), these contracts protect sensitive information shared with employees, contractors, or business partners. Confidentiality agreements ensure that the recipient of confidential information keeps it confidential and prevents unauthorized disclosure.

6. Non-Compete Agreements: These contracts restrict employees or contractors from engaging in competing activities during or after their employment or engagement with your business. Non-compete agreements help protect your business's intellectual property, trade secrets, and client relationships.

7. Service Agreements: Service agreements outline the scope of services to be provided, fees, timelines, performance expectations, and any warranties or guarantees. These contracts are commonly used by businesses in the professional services industry, such as consultants, freelancers, or agencies.

8. Partnership or Shareholder Agreements: If your business involves partnerships or multiple shareholders, these

agreements define the rights, obligations, and responsibilities of each party. They address matters such as profit distribution, decision-making processes, dispute resolution mechanisms, and exit strategies.

9. Licensing or Intellectual Property Agreements: These contracts grant or obtain rights to use or protect intellectual property, such as trademarks, copyrights, or patents. Licensing agreements define the terms and conditions of using intellectual property, while intellectual property assignment agreements transfer ownership of intellectual property from one party to another.

Each of these contracts should be tailored to the specific needs and requirements of your business. It is recommended to consult with an attorney experienced in contract law to ensure that your contracts are legally valid, comprehensive, and enforceable.

Reviewing and understanding key contract terms:

Thoroughly reviewing contracts is essential to protect your business's interests and mitigate potential risks. Here are some key steps to consider during the contract review process:

1. Read the contract carefully: Take the time to read and understand the contract in its entirety. Pay close attention to the language used, definitions of key terms, and how different sections of the contract interact with each other.

2. Identify key terms and provisions: Identify the key terms and provisions that have significant implications for your business. These may include payment terms, delivery obligations, warranties, intellectual property rights, confidentiality requirements, termination clauses, and dispute resolution mechanisms.

3. Assess potential risks: Evaluate the potential risks and liabilities associated with the contract. Consider how the contract may impact your business's financial, operational, or legal standing. Assess whether the terms are favorable and aligned with your business objectives.

4. Seek legal counsel: For complex or significant agreements, it is advisable to consult with an attorney experienced in contract law. They can provide legal advice, help identify potential pitfalls, and ensure that the contract protects your rights and interests.

5. Negotiate favorable terms: If you have concerns or want to modify certain provisions of the contract, engage in a negotiation process with the other party. Clearly communicate your concerns, propose alternative terms, and work towards reaching mutually acceptable terms that mitigate risks and align with your business goals.

6. Document all modifications: Keep a record of any modifications or amendments made to the contract during the negotiation process. Ensure that all changes are properly documented, agreed upon by all parties, and incorporated into the final contract.

7. Consider the big picture: While focusing on specific provisions, consider the overall impact of the contract on your business. Assess how the contract aligns with your long-term goals, relationships with other stakeholders, and overall risk tolerance.

8. Understand the implications of breach or termination: Familiarize yourself with the consequences of breaching or terminating the contract. Review the provisions related to termination, remedies for breach, and any associated penalties or liabilities.

9. Maintain organized contract records: Keep a well-organized system for storing and managing your contracts. Maintain copies of signed agreements, amendments, and any correspondence related to the contract. This will help facilitate future reference, contract renewals, or potential disputes.

Remember, reviewing contracts is a critical step in managing legal risks and protecting your business's interests. If you are uncertain about any aspect of a contract, seek professional legal advice to ensure that your rights and obligations are properly understood and safeguarded.

Ensuring contract enforceability and legality:

Ensuring that your contracts are legally binding and enforceable is essential to protect your business's interests. Here are some key factors to consider:

1. Voluntary agreement: Contracts must be entered into voluntarily, without any form of coercion, duress, or fraud. All parties involved should fully understand and willingly agree to the terms and conditions of the contract.
2. Offer and acceptance: A valid contract requires a clear offer by one party and an unequivocal acceptance of that offer by the

other party. The terms of the offer and acceptance must align and be mutually understood by both parties.

3. Consideration: Contracts must involve an exchange of something of value, known as consideration. This can be in the form of money, goods, services, or promises to do or refrain from doing something. Consideration is what makes the contract legally binding and distinguishes it from a mere gratuitous promise.

4. Legal capacity: Each party to a contract must have the legal capacity to enter into the agreement. This means they must be of legal age, mentally competent, and not under any legal disability or incapacity that would prevent them from understanding and fulfilling their obligations.

5. Compliance with laws and public policy: Contracts must comply with applicable laws, regulations, and public policy. Contracts that involve illegal activities, violate public policy, or contravene specific statutory requirements may be deemed unenforceable or void.

6. Clarity and specificity: Contracts should be clear, specific, and unambiguous in their terms and provisions. Vague or uncertain language can lead to misinterpretation or disputes, potentially affecting the contract's enforceability.

7. Proper documentation: Contracts should be properly documented and executed, ideally in writing, to provide a clear record of the agreement. While oral contracts can be enforceable in certain circumstances, written contracts offer greater certainty and evidentiary support.

8. Professional legal review: It is advisable to have important contracts reviewed by an experienced attorney to ensure their legal validity and enforceability. An attorney can identify potential legal issues, advise on the adequacy of the contract's terms, and help mitigate risks.

9. Compliance with formalities: Some types of contracts may require additional formalities, such as being in writing, signed by all parties, and witnessed or notarized. Familiarize yourself with any specific formalities applicable to the type of contract you are entering into.

By ensuring that your contracts meet these requirements, you can enhance their legal validity and enforceability. Consulting with a qualified attorney is highly recommended to ensure compliance with relevant laws and regulations, and to receive tailored advice based on your specific circumstances.

Resolving contract disputes and breach of agreements:

Contract disputes can be disruptive and costly for businesses. Here are some key considerations when faced with a breach of contract:

1. Open communication: In the event of a breach, open and transparent communication between the parties is crucial. Discuss the issue and attempt to resolve it amicably before escalating the situation. Sometimes, misunderstandings or miscommunications can be clarified and resolved through open dialogue.
2. Review the contract: Carefully review the terms of the contract to determine if a breach has indeed occurred. Analyze the specific obligations, conditions, and remedies outlined in the contract to assess the rights and responsibilities of each party.
3. Dispute resolution clauses: Many contracts include dispute resolution clauses that outline procedures for resolving conflicts. These clauses may require negotiation, mediation, or arbitration as a first step before resorting to litigation. Follow the procedures outlined in the contract to explore alternative dispute resolution options.
4. Negotiation: Engage in negotiations with the other party to find a mutually acceptable solution. This can involve discussions about modifying the contract, adjusting terms, or seeking compensation for damages suffered as a result of the breach.
5. Mediation: Mediation is a voluntary and confidential process where a neutral third party facilitates negotiations between the parties to help them reach a resolution. Mediation can be less adversarial and more cost-effective than litigation, and it allows the parties to maintain control over the outcome.
6. Arbitration: Arbitration is a more formal process where an impartial arbitrator or panel of arbitrators hears the case and makes a binding decision. Arbitration is typically faster and more flexible than litigation, and the rules of evidence and procedure are less formal. However, it is essential to carefully review the arbitration agreement and consider its potential advantages and disadvantages.
7. Litigation: If all attempts at resolution fail, litigation may be necessary. Engaging in a lawsuit involves presenting your case

before a court and allowing a judge or jury to make a binding decision. Litigation can be time-consuming, expensive, and emotionally taxing, so it is important to weigh the potential benefits and risks.

8. Consult an attorney: It is advisable to consult with an experienced attorney who specializes in contract law and dispute resolution. An attorney can evaluate your situation, advise you on your rights and legal options, and guide you through the dispute resolution process.

9. Preserve evidence: Keep thorough records and documentation related to the contract and the alleged breach. This includes correspondence, invoices, receipts, and any other relevant materials that can support your case.

Remember that each situation is unique, and the best course of action will depend on the specific circumstances. Consulting with an attorney will provide you with personalized advice tailored to your particular contract dispute, helping you navigate the legal complexities and seek the most favorable outcome.

Protecting intellectual property through contracts:

Safeguarding your intellectual property (IP) is crucial for protecting your business's competitive advantage and preserving the value of your intangible assets. Here are some key considerations when it comes to IP protection in contracts:

1. Non-disclosure agreements (NDAs): Include confidentiality clauses or enter into separate NDAs when sharing sensitive or proprietary information with employees, contractors, vendors, or other parties. NDAs establish a legal obligation to maintain confidentiality and prevent the unauthorized disclosure or use of confidential information.

2. Licensing agreements: If you have valuable copyrighted works, patents, trademarks, or trade secrets, consider entering into licensing agreements to establish the terms and conditions for their authorized use. Licensing agreements define the scope of the license, payment terms, restrictions, and any other relevant provisions to ensure the proper protection and monetization of your IP.

3. Ownership clauses: Clearly define ownership rights in contracts to ensure that your business retains ownership of its IP. This is especially important when collaborating with external parties,

such as contractors or consultants, who may contribute to the creation or development of intellectual property.

4. Indemnification clauses: Include indemnification provisions in contracts to protect your business from claims arising from the infringement of third-party IP rights. Such clauses may require the other party to defend, indemnify, and hold your business harmless in case of any IP-related disputes.

5. Warranty and representations: Require warranties and representations from the other party regarding the ownership or non-infringement of IP rights. This helps mitigate the risk of unknowingly entering into contracts involving IP that may be subject to third-party claims.

6. Enforcement and remedies: Specify the available remedies in the event of IP infringement or breach of contract, such as injunctive relief, damages, or termination of the agreement. Clearly outline the procedures and mechanisms for dispute resolution and the enforcement of IP rights.

7. Consult with an intellectual property attorney: Intellectual property laws can be complex and vary depending on the jurisdiction and the specific type of IP involved. Consulting with an experienced intellectual property attorney will help you understand your rights, navigate the intricacies of IP law, and ensure that your contracts adequately protect your valuable intellectual property assets.

8. Regularly review and update contracts: As your business evolves and new IP assets are developed, regularly review and update your contracts to ensure that they align with your current IP protection strategies and comply with any changes in relevant laws and regulations.

Remember, protecting your intellectual property is an ongoing process. By including the appropriate clauses in your contracts and seeking legal guidance, you can safeguard your IP rights and preserve the value of your business's intangible assets.

Creating effective vendor and client agreements:

Vendor and client agreements are essential tools for establishing successful business relationships and ensuring clarity and accountability. When drafting these agreements, consider the following key points:

1. Scope of work: Clearly define the scope of services or products to be provided by the vendor or expected from the client. Outline specific deliverables, timelines, and any performance standards or quality requirements.
2. Pricing and payment terms: Specify the agreed-upon pricing structure, payment methods, and payment terms. Include details about invoicing, due dates, late payment penalties, and any other financial arrangements. Be clear on whether pricing is fixed, variable, or subject to change based on certain factors.
3. Intellectual property ownership: Address ownership and usage rights of intellectual property in the agreement. Clarify whether the vendor retains ownership of any pre-existing IP or if the client will have ownership rights over the deliverables created during the engagement.
4. Confidentiality and data protection: Include confidentiality provisions to protect sensitive information shared between the parties. Specify the obligations to maintain confidentiality and outline any exceptions or limitations. Consider data protection requirements and compliance with applicable privacy laws.
5. Performance metrics and remedies: Define performance metrics or service-level agreements (SLAs) to measure the vendor's performance and outline remedies in case of underperformance or failure to meet agreed-upon standards. Include provisions for dispute resolution, such as mediation or arbitration, to address potential conflicts.
6. Termination and exit clauses: Clearly articulate the conditions under which either party can terminate the agreement, including any notice periods, reasons for termination, and associated rights and obligations. Address the process for transitioning services or responsibilities to another vendor or client.
7. Liability and indemnification: Allocate responsibility for liabilities, including potential damages, losses, or claims arising from the engagement. Define the extent of each party's indemnification obligations and any limitations on liability, if applicable.
8. Compliance with laws and regulations: Ensure that the agreement includes a clause stating that both parties will comply with all applicable laws, regulations, and industry standards.

9. Review and approval process: Outline the process for reviewing, revising, and approving any changes to the agreement, including the involvement of legal or authorized representatives from both parties.

Remember, each vendor or client agreement should be tailored to the specific needs and circumstances of the business relationship. It is advisable to seek legal counsel to ensure that the agreement protects your interests, aligns with your business objectives, and complies with relevant laws and regulations.

Understanding the principles of contract law is crucial for any business owner. By familiarizing yourself with key concepts such as offer and acceptance, consideration, contractual capacity, and legal purpose, you can navigate the contract creation process with confidence. This understanding allows you to draft contracts that are clear, concise, and legally binding, protecting your business's interests and minimizing the potential for disputes.

Effective contract drafting is essential for establishing mutually beneficial agreements. Clearly articulating the rights and obligations of all parties involved ensures that everyone understands their roles and responsibilities. It is important to use language that is easily understood and includes all essential terms and conditions. Engaging in negotiation processes and seeking guidance from legal professionals can help you create contracts that are fair, enforceable, and aligned with your business objectives.

Managing contractual relationships is an ongoing process that requires attention and diligence. Regularly reviewing contracts and staying informed about the implications of key terms and provisions is crucial. Paying close attention to details such as payment terms, delivery obligations, warranties, intellectual property rights, termination clauses, and dispute resolution mechanisms can help prevent misunderstandings and potential conflicts.

In complex or significant agreements, consulting with an attorney is highly recommended. Legal counsel can provide valuable insights and ensure that your contracts comply with applicable laws and regulations. They can help identify potential risks, address specific concerns, and guide you through the negotiation and drafting process to protect your business's interests.

In the event of a breach of contract or a dispute, exploring options for dispute resolution is important. Negotiation, mediation, or arbitration can provide alternative avenues for resolving conflicts outside of the courtroom. These methods often offer more cost-effective and efficient means of resolving disputes. However, in some cases, litigation may be necessary, and having the guidance of an experienced attorney can be invaluable in navigating the legal process effectively.

By understanding contract law principles, drafting contracts effectively, and managing contractual relationships with the guidance of legal professionals, you can protect your business's interests and minimize legal risks. Investing time and effort into creating solid contracts and maintaining strong relationships with your contractual partners can contribute to the long-term success of your business.

Chapter 6:

Intellectual Property Protection

Intellectual property (IP) is a valuable asset for small businesses. Understanding how to protect and enforce your IP rights is crucial in maintaining a competitive edge and safeguarding your creations. This chapter explores key concepts and strategies for intellectual property protection.

Understanding trademarks, copyrights, and patents:

Intellectual property (IP) protection is essential for businesses to safeguard their unique creations and maintain a competitive advantage. Trademarks, copyrights, and patents are three main forms of IP protection that offer legal rights and exclusivity in different areas.

Trademarks are used to protect brand names, logos, slogans, and other distinctive marks that identify and distinguish your products or services from others in the market. Registering a trademark provides legal recognition and ownership, allowing you to prevent others from using similar marks that could cause confusion among consumers. By securing trademark protection, you can establish a strong brand identity and build customer trust.

Copyrights protect original works of authorship, including literature, music, artwork, photographs, and software. This protection grants exclusive rights to the creator or owner, preventing others from reproducing, distributing, or displaying the copyrighted work without permission. Registering a copyright strengthens your legal position and allows you to pursue legal remedies in case of infringement, ensuring that you have control over the use and distribution of your creative works.

Patents are a form of protection for inventions, processes, or new technology. They grant the inventor exclusive rights to make, use, or sell the patented invention for a limited period. Patents encourage innovation by providing inventors with the opportunity to profit from their inventions and prevent others from using or commercializing the same technology. Obtaining a patent involves a thorough application process and requires meeting specific criteria of novelty, non-obviousness, and usefulness.

It is important to consult with an intellectual property attorney to determine the most appropriate form of protection for your business and to navigate the complex process of filing for trademarks, copyrights, or patents. They can guide you through the application process, conduct searches to ensure your IP does not infringe on existing rights, and help enforce your IP rights if infringement occurs.

By securing intellectual property protection, you can safeguard your brand, creative works, and innovations, and protect the value and integrity of your business. It is an investment that can provide long-term benefits and prevent unauthorized use or exploitation of your intellectual assets by others.

Conducting comprehensive intellectual property searches:

Before embarking on branding initiatives or developing new products, it is crucial to conduct comprehensive searches to determine if your chosen name, logo, or invention infringes upon existing intellectual property (IP) rights. This proactive step helps you minimize the risk of potential legal disputes and infringement claims.

Conducting IP searches involves researching various databases, online platforms, and resources to identify existing trademarks, copyrights, and patents that may be similar or identical to your proposed IP. These searches aim to uncover any potential conflicts or similarities that could lead to confusion among consumers or infringe upon the rights of others.

Online databases, such as the United States Patent and Trademark Office (USPTO) database or the World Intellectual Property Organization (WIPO) database, provide valuable information on registered trademarks and patents. Additionally, conducting internet searches, reviewing trade directories, and consulting with IP professionals can help identify any unregistered or common-law trademarks that may pose a risk.

Engaging the services of an IP attorney or professional can provide valuable expertise and guidance during the search process. They can help interpret search results, assess the likelihood of conflicts, and provide advice on potential risks and mitigation strategies. They can also assist in determining if your proposed IP is distinctive enough to be registered and offer guidance on strengthening your IP position.

By conducting thorough IP searches, you can identify potential conflicts early on and make informed decisions regarding your branding, marketing, and product development strategies. This proactive approach not only helps protect your business from potential legal disputes but also ensures that your brand and products have a clear and distinct identity in the marketplace.

Remember, IP rights are valuable assets that contribute to the success and reputation of your business. Taking the necessary steps to ensure your IP does not infringe upon the rights of others demonstrates your commitment to ethical business practices and protects the investments you make in developing your brand and products.

Registering trademarks with the USPTO:

Registering your trademarks with the United States Patent and Trademark Office (USPTO) offers significant benefits and legal protections for your brand. Federal trademark registration provides exclusive rights to use the mark in connection with your products or services throughout the United States.

By registering your trademarks, you establish a legal presumption of ownership and acquire nationwide recognition and protection. This means that others are on notice of your rights, reducing the likelihood of unintentional infringement. It also provides a strong basis for legal action against infringers, allowing you to enforce your trademark rights and protect your brand reputation.

The process of trademark registration can be complex, requiring a thorough understanding of trademark law and the application requirements. It is advisable to consult with a trademark attorney who specializes in intellectual property to guide you through the application process effectively. They can help conduct a comprehensive trademark search, assess the strength of your mark, and prepare and file the necessary application documents.

A trademark attorney can also assist in navigating potential obstacles or challenges during the registration process, such as responding to office actions or overcoming objections from the USPTO. Their expertise ensures that your application meets all legal requirements and increases the likelihood of successful registration.

Registering your trademarks with the USPTO demonstrates your commitment to protecting your brand and its distinctive identity. It provides valuable legal protection, strengthens your position in the marketplace, and enhances the value of your business assets. By consulting with a trademark attorney and following the proper registration process, you can safeguard your trademarks and enjoy the benefits of federal protection.

Protecting copyrights and fair use considerations:

Copyright protection is automatically granted to original works of authorship upon their creation. This protection extends to various forms of creative expression, such as literary works, music, artwork, photographs, and software. While registration with the U.S. Copyright Office is not required for protection, it offers important benefits and strengthens your legal position.

By registering your works with the U.S. Copyright Office, you establish a public record of your ownership and create a presumption of validity for your copyrights. This is particularly valuable in situations where disputes or infringement claims arise, as it simplifies the process of asserting your rights and pursuing legal remedies.

Registering your works also grants you the ability to bring a lawsuit for copyright infringement in federal court. Without registration, you may be limited to seeking only actual damages, whereas registration allows you to pursue statutory damages and attorney's fees.

Furthermore, registering your works can act as a deterrent to potential infringers. When your works bear the copyright symbol (©) and are accompanied by a copyright registration, it sends a clear message that you are serious about protecting your intellectual property and may discourage unauthorized use.

It is important to understand the concept of fair use, which allows for limited use of copyrighted works without obtaining permission from the copyright owner. Fair use is a legal doctrine that allows for uses such as commentary, criticism, news reporting, teaching, and research. However, the determination of fair use is fact-specific and depends on various factors, such as the purpose and nature of the use, the amount and substantiality of the portion used, and the effect on the market for the original work.

To protect your copyrighted materials and deter infringement, consider implementing strategies such as using watermarks or digital rights management tools for digital content, including copyright notices on your works, monitoring for unauthorized use, and pursuing legal action when necessary.

Consulting with an intellectual property attorney can provide you with comprehensive guidance on copyright protection, fair use, and enforcement strategies. They can assist you in navigating the registration process and developing a tailored approach to protect your creative works effectively.

Safeguarding trade secrets and confidential information:

Trade secrets are valuable intellectual assets that can provide a competitive edge to businesses. Unlike patents, trademarks, or copyrights, trade secrets rely on their secrecy to maintain their value. To protect your trade secrets, it is essential to implement robust confidentiality measures.

One effective way to safeguard trade secrets is by using confidentiality agreements, also known as non-disclosure agreements (NDAs). These agreements establish a legal framework for protecting confidential information and preventing its unauthorized disclosure. NDAs should be tailored to the specific needs of your business and clearly define the confidential information, the parties involved, the purpose of disclosure, and the obligations of the recipient to maintain confidentiality.

In addition to confidentiality agreements, it is important to restrict access to trade secrets on a need-to-know basis. Limiting access to only those employees, vendors, or partners who require the information to perform their duties reduces the risk of unauthorized disclosure. Implementing physical and digital security measures, such as password protection, encryption, and restricted access controls, further enhances the protection of trade secrets.

Establishing clear protocols and guidelines for employees, vendors, and partners is crucial for maintaining the confidentiality of trade secrets. This includes training employees on the importance of confidentiality, regularly reviewing and updating security measures, and enforcing strict internal policies regarding the handling and storage of confidential information.

It is also important to conduct regular audits to identify potential vulnerabilities and ensure compliance with confidentiality protocols. Monitoring and detecting any unauthorized access or breaches can help mitigate the risk of trade secret misappropriation.

If a trade secret is misappropriated, swift and decisive action is necessary. This may involve pursuing legal remedies, such as injunctions or damages, against the parties responsible for the unauthorized disclosure or use of the trade secret.

Consulting with an intellectual property attorney who specializes in trade secrets can provide valuable guidance on how to identify, protect, and enforce your trade secrets effectively. They can assist in developing comprehensive strategies to safeguard your confidential information and preserve your competitive advantage.

Avoiding infringement and understanding licensing:

Conducting due diligence is crucial to avoid infringing on the intellectual property (IP) rights of others. Intellectual property infringement can result in legal disputes, financial penalties, and damage to your business's reputation. To mitigate these risks, it is important to seek legal counsel and assess potential IP issues before using copyrighted materials or leveraging patented technologies.

When using copyrighted materials, such as images, music, or written content, it is important to understand the scope of copyright protection and any applicable limitations, such as fair use exceptions. Consulting with an intellectual property attorney can help you determine whether your intended use falls within the bounds of fair use or whether you need to obtain permission from the copyright owner.

In the case of patented technologies, it is essential to conduct a thorough patent search to ensure that your proposed use or product does not infringe on existing patents. An experienced patent attorney can assist you in conducting a comprehensive search and analyzing the patent landscape to identify any potential risks. If there are concerns about patent infringement, licensing agreements can be pursued to obtain permission from the patent holder to use their technology under specific terms and conditions.

Licensing agreements grant you the legal right to use someone else's intellectual property while ensuring compliance with their terms. These agreements outline the scope of the license, any restrictions or limitations, payment terms, and other important considerations. Working with an attorney experienced in intellectual property licensing can help you negotiate and draft licensing agreements that protect your interests and ensure compliance with the terms set forth by the IP owner.

By conducting due diligence and obtaining appropriate licenses when necessary, you can minimize the risk of infringing on others' intellectual property rights and protect your business from legal complications. Legal counsel can provide valuable guidance throughout the process, helping you navigate complex IP issues and avoid costly disputes.

Enforcing intellectual property rights and legal remedies:

In the event that someone infringes upon your intellectual property rights, there are legal remedies available to protect your rights and seek appropriate compensation.

One common initial step is to send a cease and desist letter to the infringing party. This letter formally notifies them of the infringement and demands that they immediately stop using your intellectual property. Cease and desist letters can often lead to resolution without the need for further legal action.

If negotiations or a cease and desist letter do not resolve the dispute, alternative dispute resolution methods like mediation or arbitration can be pursued. These processes provide a structured and facilitated environment for parties to discuss their concerns and work towards a mutually acceptable resolution with the assistance of a neutral third party. Mediation and arbitration can be more cost-effective and time-efficient than traditional litigation.

However, in more severe cases or when resolution cannot be reached through negotiation or alternative dispute resolution, litigation may be necessary. Litigation involves filing a lawsuit in court to protect your rights and seek damages or injunctive relief. It is important to consult with an intellectual property attorney to assess the strength of your case, evaluate the potential remedies available, and determine the best course of action.

Intellectual property litigation can be complex and costly, so it is important to carefully consider the potential benefits and risks before proceeding. An experienced intellectual property attorney can guide you through the legal process, represent your interests, and help you navigate the complexities of intellectual property litigation.

Ultimately, the appropriate course of action will depend on the specific circumstances of your case. Consulting with an attorney who specializes in intellectual property law is crucial to determine the most effective strategy for enforcing your intellectual property rights and protecting your business's interests.

Navigating intellectual property disputes:

Engaging with specialized intellectual property attorneys is crucial when dealing with intellectual property disputes. These attorneys have expertise in the intricacies of intellectual property law and can provide valuable guidance throughout the dispute resolution process.

Intellectual property attorneys can carefully analyze the facts and circumstances of your case to assess the strength of your intellectual property rights and the potential infringement. They can help you understand your legal rights and options, as well as the potential risks and benefits associated with different courses of action.

In intellectual property disputes, settlement negotiations are often a preferred method of resolving the issue without resorting to litigation. Intellectual property attorneys can represent your interests in negotiations, working to reach a favorable settlement that protects your rights and satisfies your objectives. They can guide you through the negotiation process, ensuring that your rights are properly represented and that any settlement agreements are legally sound.

If settlement negotiations are unsuccessful, intellectual property attorneys can help prepare and present infringement claims or defenses in legal proceedings. They have the knowledge and experience to navigate the complexities of intellectual property litigation, including gathering evidence, drafting legal documents, and presenting arguments in court. They can advocate for your interests and work to achieve a favorable outcome.

Throughout the dispute resolution process, intellectual property attorneys can provide strategic advice tailored to your specific situation. They can help you weigh the costs and benefits of different approaches, assess the risks involved, and make informed decisions. Their expertise and experience can significantly enhance your chances of successfully resolving the dispute and protecting your intellectual property rights.

By engaging with specialized intellectual property attorneys, you can ensure that your interests are effectively represented, increase the likelihood of a favorable resolution, and minimize the potential impact of the dispute on your business.

Understanding the intricacies of intellectual property protection is crucial for preserving the value of your IP assets. By conducting thorough searches and due diligence, you can minimize the risk of infringing on others' intellectual property rights and identify potential conflicts early on.

Registering your trademarks with the appropriate intellectual property offices provides legal recognition and strengthens your rights. Consult with trademark attorneys to navigate the registration process and ensure your trademarks are properly protected.

Implementing strategies to safeguard your intellectual property, such as using confidentiality agreements (NDAs), securing trade secrets, and monitoring unauthorized use, helps protect your creations and maintain a competitive edge. Intellectual property attorneys can assist in drafting and enforcing these agreements and provide guidance on best practices for safeguarding your intellectual property.

In the event of a dispute or infringement, engaging with intellectual property professionals, such as attorneys specializing in intellectual property law, is essential. These professionals have the knowledge and experience to analyze the situation, assess the strength of your intellectual property rights, and advise you on the appropriate course of action.

Intellectual property professionals can assist in negotiating settlements, preparing infringement claims, and representing your interests in legal proceedings. They can navigate the complexities of intellectual property disputes, gather evidence, present arguments, and work towards a favorable resolution.

It is important to consult with intellectual property professionals who are well-versed in the specific laws and regulations governing intellectual property in your jurisdiction. They can provide personalized guidance tailored to your business and help you develop a comprehensive strategy to protect and enforce your intellectual property rights.

By understanding and protecting your intellectual property assets, you can safeguard your competitive advantage, preserve the value of your creations, and ensure that your business remains protected in a rapidly evolving marketplace.

Chapter 7:

Marketing and Advertising Compliance

Marketing and advertising play a crucial role in promoting your small business. However, it is essential to understand the legal considerations surrounding marketing activities to ensure compliance and maintain trust with consumers. This chapter explores key aspects of marketing and advertising compliance.

Understanding legal considerations for advertising:

Familiarizing yourself with laws and regulations governing advertising is essential for building credibility and maintaining ethical business practices. It is important to understand both federal and state guidelines that govern advertising activities.

The Federal Trade Commission (FTC) Act is a key federal law that regulates advertising practices in the United States. It prohibits deceptive or unfair trade practices, including false or misleading advertising, fraudulent claims, and unfair competition. Adhering to the FTC Act ensures that your advertising is truthful, transparent, and does not mislead consumers.

In addition to federal laws, it is crucial to be aware of state-specific advertising regulations. Some states may have additional requirements or restrictions on certain industries or types of advertising. Research and comply with the advertising laws and regulations in the states where you conduct business to ensure full compliance.

When creating advertisements, it is important to make accurate claims about your products or services, provide clear and complete information, and avoid any deceptive or misleading statements. Claims should be supported by substantiated evidence, and any disclaimers or disclosures should be prominently displayed and easily understandable.

Transparency is key in advertising. Clearly identify any sponsored content or paid endorsements to avoid misleading consumers. Disclose any material connections with endorsers or influencers in accordance with the FTC guidelines.

It is advisable to keep up-to-date with the latest developments in advertising regulations. The FTC provides resources and guidelines on its website that can help you stay informed about advertising best practices and compliance requirements.

Consulting with an attorney experienced in advertising law or seeking guidance from a compliance professional can provide valuable insights and help ensure that your advertising practices are in line with legal requirements and industry standards.

By understanding and complying with advertising laws and regulations, you not only protect consumers but also build trust and credibility with your audience, enhancing the reputation and success of your business.

Complying with FTC regulations and guidelines:

The Federal Trade Commission (FTC) plays a crucial role in enforcing regulations that govern advertising, marketing, and consumer protection in the United States. Familiarizing yourself with FTC guidelines is important to ensure compliance and maintain transparency in your advertising practices.

One key area of FTC guidelines relates to endorsements and testimonials. If you use endorsements or testimonials in your advertising, it is essential to disclose any material connections between the endorser and your business. This includes relationships such as receiving payment or free products in exchange for the endorsement. The disclosure should be clear and conspicuous, ensuring that consumers are aware of any potential bias.

Native advertising is another area covered by FTC guidelines. Native ads are designed to resemble non-advertising content and can sometimes blur the line between advertising and editorial content. The FTC requires clear and prominent disclosure when native ads are used to ensure that consumers can easily distinguish between advertising and non-advertising content.

The FTC also emphasizes the importance of clear and conspicuous disclosures in all forms of advertising. Disclosures should be placed where consumers are likely to see them and should use language that is easy to understand. Whether it's disclosing the terms and conditions of a promotion or providing information about potential risks or side effects of a product, clear and conspicuous disclosures help prevent misleading or deceptive practices.

Complying with FTC guidelines is not only a legal requirement but also a way to build trust with consumers. By being transparent in your advertising practices and providing accurate information, you can establish credibility and maintain positive relationships with your customers.

It is advisable to regularly review and stay updated on FTC guidelines, as they may evolve to address emerging trends and technologies in advertising. The FTC website provides resources, guides, and examples that can help you understand and implement these guidelines effectively.

Working with legal counsel or consulting with professionals who specialize in advertising compliance can provide valuable insights and guidance specific to your industry and advertising practices.

By understanding and adhering to FTC guidelines, you demonstrate a commitment to ethical advertising, protect consumers from deceptive practices, and maintain the integrity of your business.

Truth in advertising and avoiding deceptive practices:

Maintaining honesty and integrity in your marketing materials is crucial to build trust with consumers. It is important to ensure that your marketing claims are truthful, accurate, and not misleading.

Avoid making false claims or exaggerating the benefits or performance of your products or services. Any statements you make should be supported by objective evidence or scientific data. This evidence should be reliable, current, and relevant to the specific claims being made. If you are using statistics or research data, ensure that it is properly attributed and accurately represents the information being presented.

Transparency is key when providing information about your products or services. Clearly disclose any limitations, restrictions, or conditions associated with your offerings. This includes any potential risks, side effects, or prerequisites for using or benefiting from your products or services. Providing consumers with complete and accurate information allows them to make informed decisions and reduces the risk of misunderstandings or disappointment.

It is important to avoid deceptive practices such as bait-and-switch tactics or hidden fees. Ensure that your pricing, discounts, and offers are clearly communicated and accurately represented. Any terms or conditions associated with your marketing promotions should be easily accessible and clearly stated.

In addition to the FTC guidelines, be aware of any industry-specific regulations or self-regulatory codes that apply to your business. For example, certain industries like healthcare or financial services may have additional guidelines or requirements to ensure responsible and ethical marketing practices.

Regularly review and update your marketing materials to ensure ongoing compliance with legal and ethical standards. As your business evolves and new products or services are introduced, it is important to assess the accuracy and appropriateness of your marketing claims.

By maintaining honesty, accuracy, and transparency in your marketing materials, you can build a strong reputation, foster trust with consumers, and establish long-lasting relationships with your target audience.

Understanding email marketing and spam laws:

When conducting email marketing campaigns, it is essential to comply with relevant spam laws, such as the CAN-SPAM Act (Controlling the Assault of Non-Solicited Pornography And Marketing Act). This act sets guidelines for commercial email communications and aims to protect consumers from unwanted spam emails.

To ensure compliance with the CAN-SPAM Act, follow these key practices:

1. Accurate Sender Information: Provide accurate and identifiable sender information in your emails. Include your company's name, physical address, and contact information. This helps recipients recognize the sender and establishes transparency.
2. Opt-Out or Unsubscribe Option: Include a clear and conspicuous option for recipients to unsubscribe from your email list. Honor unsubscribe requests promptly and remove those individuals from your mailing list within 10 business days.
3. Identification of Commercial Content: Clearly indicate that your email contains commercial content. This can be done through a proper subject line that accurately reflects the nature of the email. Additionally, ensure that the body of the email clearly identifies it as an advertisement or promotional material.
4. Consent-Based Email Lists: Obtain the consent of recipients before sending them commercial emails. This can be done

through explicit opt-in mechanisms, such as checkboxes on website forms or confirmation emails. Keep records of consent to demonstrate compliance if required.

5. Monitoring Third-Party Service Providers: If you use a third-party service provider for email marketing, ensure that they also comply with applicable spam laws. Regularly monitor and audit their practices to maintain compliance.

6. Timely Processing of Opt-Out Requests: Honor unsubscribe requests promptly. Once a recipient requests to be removed from your email list, ensure they no longer receive commercial emails from your business.

7. Regular Review and Compliance Maintenance: Regularly review and update your email marketing practices to ensure ongoing compliance with spam laws. Stay informed about any changes in regulations and best practices.

By adhering to these practices, you can maintain compliance with spam laws, build trust with your email recipients, and promote responsible and ethical email marketing practices.

Implementing data privacy and protection measures:

Protecting consumer data and complying with data privacy laws is crucial for maintaining trust and avoiding legal issues. Here are some key steps to consider:

1. Understand Applicable Laws: Familiarize yourself with data privacy laws that apply to your business, such as the General Data Protection Regulation (GDPR) if you have customers in the European Union. Be aware of your obligations and requirements under these laws.

2. Data Collection and Consent: Obtain explicit consent from individuals before collecting their personal data. Clearly inform them about the purpose of data collection, how the data will be used, and any third parties involved. Allow individuals to easily withdraw their consent if desired.

3. Data Security Measures: Implement appropriate data security measures to protect consumer data from unauthorized access, loss, or theft. This can include using encryption, secure servers, firewalls, and access controls. Regularly review and update your security practices to address emerging threats.

4. Privacy Policy and Notices: Create a comprehensive and easily accessible privacy policy that outlines your data collection, use,

and sharing practices. Make sure it is written in clear and understandable language. Provide individuals with clear and concise notices regarding data collection at the time of collection.

5. Data Retention and Deletion: Establish policies and procedures for the retention and deletion of personal data. Only retain data for as long as necessary and securely dispose of it when no longer needed.

6. Third-Party Data Processors: If you share personal data with third-party service providers or processors, ensure that they have appropriate data protection measures in place. Enter into agreements that outline the responsibilities and obligations of both parties in safeguarding data.

7. Individual Rights: Respect individuals' rights regarding their personal data. Provide mechanisms for individuals to access, correct, or delete their data, as well as the ability to opt out of marketing communications.

8. Employee Training and Awareness: Educate your employees about data privacy practices and their roles in protecting consumer data. Ensure they understand the importance of privacy and are trained to handle data securely.

9. Regular Audits and Compliance Reviews: Conduct periodic audits and reviews of your data privacy practices to ensure ongoing compliance with applicable laws. Stay updated on any changes in regulations and adjust your practices accordingly.

By implementing these measures, you can protect consumer data, comply with data privacy laws, and demonstrate your commitment to safeguarding customer privacy. Prioritize data privacy as an integral part of your business operations to build trust with your customers.

Creating compliant marketing materials and disclosures:

When creating marketing materials, it's important to ensure compliance with legal requirements. Here are some key considerations:

1. Truthful and Accurate Information: Present information about your products or services in a truthful, accurate, and non-deceptive manner. Avoid making false claims or misrepresentations that could mislead consumers.

2. Material Information: Disclose all material information that could affect consumers' purchasing decisions. This includes pricing, terms and conditions, any limitations or restrictions,

and any additional fees or charges. Ensure that this information is clear, prominent, and easily understandable.

3. Clear and Conspicuous Disclosures: Use clear and conspicuous language when including disclosures in your marketing materials. Disclosures should be easily noticeable and not hidden or buried in fine print. Consider the size, color, placement, and format of the disclosures to ensure they are effectively communicated to consumers.

4. Disclaimers: Include appropriate disclaimers to clarify the scope, limitations, or potential risks associated with your products or services. Make sure these disclaimers are clearly visible and prominent, providing consumers with necessary information to make informed decisions.

5. Endorsements and Testimonials: If your marketing materials include endorsements or testimonials, comply with FTC guidelines. Ensure that any material connections between endorsers and your business are disclosed, and that the opinions expressed are honest and representative of actual experiences.

6. Comparative Advertising: If you engage in comparative advertising, ensure that any comparisons made are truthful, accurate, and substantiated. Avoid making false or misleading statements about your competitors or their products.

7. Regulatory Compliance: Stay up to date with applicable advertising regulations, such as those set forth by the Federal Trade Commission (FTC) and other relevant agencies. Understand the specific guidelines and requirements that apply to your industry or type of advertising.

8. Review by Legal Professionals: Consider having your marketing materials reviewed by legal professionals who specialize in advertising and marketing law. They can provide guidance and ensure compliance with applicable regulations.

9. Ongoing Compliance Monitoring: Regularly review and update your marketing materials to ensure ongoing compliance with legal requirements. Stay informed about changes in regulations and adjust your marketing strategies accordingly.

By developing marketing materials that comply with legal requirements, you can build trust with consumers, maintain a positive reputation, and avoid potential legal issues.

Intellectual property considerations in marketing:

When creating marketing materials, it's important to respect the intellectual property rights of others. Here are some key considerations:

1. Trademarks: Avoid using trademarks, logos, or brand names that belong to others without permission. Conduct thorough searches to ensure that your marketing materials do not infringe on existing trademark rights. If you need to use a trademark, seek appropriate licensing or obtain permission from the trademark owner.

2. Copyrighted Materials: Do not use copyrighted materials, such as images, text, or music, without obtaining the necessary permissions or licenses. Be aware of fair use exceptions, which allow limited use of copyrighted materials for specific purposes such as commentary, criticism, or education. When in doubt, consult with legal professionals or obtain proper licenses to ensure compliance.

3. Licensing Agreements: If you wish to use someone else's intellectual property, such as copyrighted materials or patented technologies, explore licensing agreements. Licensing agreements grant you permission to use the intellectual property of others while ensuring compliance with their terms and conditions. Consult with legal professionals to negotiate and draft appropriate licensing agreements.

4. Original Content Creation: Focus on creating original marketing materials to avoid infringing on the intellectual property rights of others. Develop unique branding, designs, and content that reflect your business and differentiate you from competitors. This helps protect your own intellectual property rights while showcasing your originality.

5. Intellectual Property Searches: Conduct searches to identify existing intellectual property rights related to your marketing materials. Use online databases, search engines, or consult with intellectual property professionals to ensure that your materials do not infringe on others' rights.

6. Monitoring and Enforcement: Regularly monitor your marketing materials to ensure ongoing compliance with intellectual property laws. Stay informed about changes in trademarks, copyrights, or patents that could impact your materials. If you discover any infringement claims against your business, address them promptly and seek legal advice if necessary.

By respecting intellectual property rights and obtaining proper permissions or licenses, you can create marketing materials that are legally compliant, ethically sound, and reflective of your brand's integrity.

Navigating social media and influencer marketing guidelines:

When engaging in social media and influencer marketing, it's important to comply with the Federal Trade Commission (FTC) guidelines regarding disclosures. Here are some key considerations:

1. Sponsored Content: If you collaborate with influencers or individuals to promote your products or services, ensure that they disclose their relationship with your business. Disclosures should be clear, conspicuous, and easily noticeable to consumers. Use terms like "Sponsored," "Paid partnership," or "Advertisement" to indicate the commercial nature of the content.

2. Endorsements and Testimonials: If you feature endorsements or testimonials from customers or influencers, ensure that they reflect the genuine opinions and experiences of the individuals involved. Disclose any material connections between the endorser and your business to provide transparency to consumers.

3. Material Connections: Disclose any material connections between your business and influencers, such as financial arrangements, free products, or other incentives. These disclosures help consumers understand the potential bias or incentives that may influence the endorsement or content.

4. Placement and Visibility: Ensure that disclosures are placed in a location where consumers can easily see them, such as at the beginning of social media posts or in close proximity to endorsements. Disclosures should not be buried in a long list of hashtags or hidden within the content.

5. Education and Monitoring: Educate influencers and endorsers about the FTC guidelines and the importance of proper disclosures. Monitor their content to ensure compliance with the guidelines and provide guidance or reminders as needed.

6. Review Contracts and Agreements: When working with influencers or endorsers, include clear language in contracts or agreements outlining the requirement for proper disclosures.

Review the content created by influencers to ensure compliance with the agreed-upon disclosure requirements.

By adhering to the FTC guidelines and ensuring proper disclosures in social media and influencer marketing, you can maintain transparency, build trust with consumers, and comply with legal requirements. Regularly stay informed about updates or changes in the guidelines to ensure ongoing compliance.

By understanding and adhering to legal considerations in marketing and advertising, you can build trust with consumers, maintain compliance with regulations, and avoid legal disputes. The field of marketing and advertising is subject to various laws and regulations that govern fair competition, consumer protection, and truthful advertising practices. As an attorney, it is crucial to guide clients in understanding and navigating these legal requirements.

One important legal consideration is the Federal Trade Commission (FTC) Act, which prohibits deceptive or unfair trade practices. This Act establishes guidelines that businesses must follow to ensure their marketing and advertising activities are truthful and not misleading. Familiarize yourself with the FTC guidelines and advise clients on how to comply with them.

Transparency is a key principle in marketing and advertising. Provide clear and accurate information about your products or services, avoiding false or exaggerated claims that could mislead consumers. Ensure that marketing materials, including websites, social media posts, and advertisements, are truthful, substantiated, and not deceptive.

Disclosures play a vital role in maintaining transparency. Disclosures provide additional information to consumers, such as material terms, limitations, or disclaimers, that may impact their purchasing decisions. The placement, visibility, and clarity of disclosures are crucial to ensure consumers can easily understand and access them. Review and advise clients on appropriate disclosure practices based on the specific context and medium of their marketing activities.

When using endorsements or testimonials, ensure that they reflect the genuine opinions and experiences of the individuals involved. Any material connections or incentives between endorsers and the business should be disclosed to consumers. Advise clients on the proper use of endorsements and testimonials to ensure compliance with the FTC guidelines.

When engaging in digital marketing, such as email marketing or online behavioral advertising, be aware of applicable laws and regulations, such as the CAN-SPAM Act and the use of cookies for tracking purposes. Understand the requirements for obtaining consent, providing opt-out options, and honoring consumer preferences regarding data collection and marketing communications.

Privacy is another important aspect of marketing and advertising. Comply with data protection laws and regulations, such as the General Data Protection Regulation (GDPR), when collecting, storing, and using personal data. Implement appropriate security measures to protect consumer data and ensure compliance with privacy requirements.

Review and update your marketing practices regularly to align with evolving laws and regulations. Stay informed about new legal developments, guidelines, and best practices in the marketing and advertising field. Consult with legal professionals experienced in marketing and advertising law to obtain guidance and advice specific to your clients' needs.

By providing legal guidance on marketing and advertising practices, you can assist businesses in maintaining compliance, mitigating legal risks, and promoting ethical advertising practices. Help your clients build a strong and reputable brand while adhering to legal standards and consumer protection principles.

Chapter 8:

Online Business and E-commerce

The digital landscape offers vast opportunities for small businesses to reach a wider audience and engage in e-commerce. However, navigating the online realm requires understanding legal considerations specific to online business and e-commerce activities. This chapter explores key aspects of establishing and operating an online business.

Establishing an online presence and website legal compliance:

When establishing an online presence, it is crucial to ensure that your website complies with applicable laws and regulations. Displaying clear terms of service, a privacy policy, and disclaimers helps set expectations and establishes the contractual relationship between the website and its users. These legal documents should address important aspects such as user responsibilities, limitations of liability, and dispute resolution mechanisms.

Intellectual property considerations are also essential for online businesses. Ensure that your website respects the intellectual property rights of others by addressing copyright notices, trademarks, and restrictions on the use of content. Obtain necessary licenses or permissions when using copyrighted materials or trademarks belonging to third parties.

Privacy protection is of utmost importance in the online environment. Create and prominently display a privacy policy that outlines how personal information is collected, used, stored, and shared. Comply with relevant data protection laws, such as the General Data Protection Regulation (GDPR), and obtain proper consent for the collection and processing of personal data.

Inclusivity is a key aspect of online accessibility. Ensure that your website is accessible to individuals with disabilities, complying with accessibility requirements such as those outlined in the Americans with Disabilities Act (ADA) and Web Content Accessibility Guidelines (WCAG). This may involve providing alternative text for images, keyboard navigation options, and captioning for videos, among other accessibility features.

Regularly review and update your website's legal documentation to reflect any changes in laws, regulations, or business practices. Consult with legal professionals experienced in internet and e-commerce law to ensure compliance with applicable legal requirements and best practices.

By taking the necessary steps to comply with laws and regulations, you can establish a trustworthy online presence, protect the rights of others, and mitigate legal risks associated with online activities. Safeguarding the legal integrity of your website builds credibility and fosters positive relationships with users and customers.

Understanding online consumer protection laws:

When conducting online transactions, it is essential to familiarize yourself with consumer protection laws that govern these transactions. The Federal Trade Commission Act (FTC Act) is a key federal law that prohibits deceptive and unfair trade practices. Additionally, each state may have its own consumer protection statutes that apply to online transactions.

To ensure compliance with consumer protection laws, provide accurate and transparent product information on your website. Clearly state the pricing of your products or services, including any applicable taxes or fees. Avoid false or misleading representations about the quality, features, or benefits of your products.

Having a fair return and refund policy is important to instill confidence in your customers. Clearly communicate your policy and ensure that it complies with applicable laws, such as allowing for reasonable timeframes and providing refunds or exchanges when appropriate.

Honoring consumer privacy rights is also crucial. Protect the personal information you collect from customers and clearly communicate your data privacy practices. Obtain proper consent for the collection, use, and sharing of personal data and ensure compliance with relevant privacy laws, such as the GDPR or the California Consumer Privacy Act (CCPA).

Stay informed about changes and updates in consumer protection laws to ensure ongoing compliance. Consult with legal professionals specializing in consumer protection laws to review your practices and ensure adherence to applicable regulations.

By prioritizing consumer protection in your online transactions, you demonstrate a commitment to ethical business practices and build trust with your customers. Complying with consumer protection laws helps mitigate legal risks and fosters positive relationships with your online consumers.

Complying with privacy and data protection regulations:

Safeguarding consumer data and complying with privacy laws is of paramount importance in today's digital landscape. If your business collects and processes personal data, it is crucial to understand and adhere to privacy laws such as the General Data Protection Regulation (GDPR) or the California Consumer Privacy Act (CCPA), depending on your jurisdiction and the location of your customers.

To comply with these laws, obtain informed and explicit consent from individuals before collecting and using their personal data. Clearly communicate the purposes for which the data will be used, the types of data collected, and any third parties with whom the data may be shared. Implement appropriate security measures to protect the data from unauthorized access, loss, or disclosure.

Transparency is key in privacy compliance. Provide a comprehensive privacy policy that clearly explains your data practices, including how individuals can exercise their rights, such as the right to access, correct, or delete their personal data. Ensure that your privacy policy is easily accessible on your website and regularly updated to reflect any changes in your data handling practices.

If your business operates in multiple jurisdictions, be aware of the specific requirements and obligations imposed by each applicable privacy law. This may include appointing a data protection officer, conducting data protection impact assessments, or maintaining records of data processing activities.

Regularly review and assess your data handling practices to ensure ongoing compliance with privacy laws. Seek legal counsel or engage privacy professionals to conduct privacy audits and provide guidance on privacy compliance.

By safeguarding consumer data and complying with privacy laws, you demonstrate your commitment to protecting individuals' privacy rights and building trust with your customers. It also helps mitigate the risk of data breaches, regulatory penalties, and reputational damage associated with non-compliance.

Implementing secure online payment systems:

Ensuring secure online transactions is crucial for maintaining the trust and confidence of your customers. Implementing trusted and reliable payment systems is an essential step in this process. Choose payment service providers that have a strong reputation for security and compliance with industry standards.

Complying with the Payment Card Industry Data Security Standard (PCI DSS) is particularly important for businesses that handle credit card transactions. The PCI DSS provides a set of security requirements that businesses must follow to protect cardholder data. It covers areas such as secure network architecture, access controls, encryption, vulnerability management, and regular monitoring and testing.

To comply with PCI DSS requirements, ensure that sensitive cardholder data is encrypted during transmission and storage. Use secure protocols for online transactions, such as Transport Layer Security (TLS), to protect data in transit. Implement robust access controls to limit access to cardholder data only to authorized personnel. Regularly update and patch your systems to address vulnerabilities and conduct regular security assessments and penetration testing.

Maintaining a secure payment gateway is also essential. The payment gateway is the interface between your website and the payment processor, and it is responsible for securely transmitting payment data. Choose a reputable payment gateway provider that employs strong security measures, such as tokenization or point-to-point encryption, to protect customer payment information.

Regularly review and update your security measures to stay ahead of emerging threats and vulnerabilities. Stay informed about industry best practices and any updates to security standards. Engage with security professionals or consult with a qualified IT team to conduct regular security assessments and ensure ongoing compliance with PCI DSS and other relevant security standards.

By implementing trusted and secure payment systems, complying with industry standards such as PCI DSS, and regularly updating your security measures, you can protect customer payment information and provide a safe online transaction experience. Demonstrating a commitment to data security not only protects your customers but also enhances your reputation and builds trust in your business.

Protecting against cyber threats and fraud:

Developing robust cybersecurity measures is crucial in today's digital landscape to protect your online business and customer information from cyber threats and fraud. Implementing a multi-layered approach to cybersecurity can significantly enhance your defenses.

Start by deploying firewalls, which act as a barrier between your internal network and the internet, monitoring and filtering incoming and outgoing traffic. Configure firewalls to restrict unauthorized access and block potential threats. Additionally, regularly update and patch your firewall software to address any known vulnerabilities.

Complement your firewall with reliable antivirus and anti-malware software. These programs can detect and remove malicious software, including viruses, worms, and ransomware, from your systems. Ensure that antivirus software is regularly updated to defend against the latest threats.

Implement intrusion detection systems (IDS) or intrusion prevention systems (IPS) to monitor network traffic and detect suspicious activity or unauthorized access attempts. IDS/IPS can alert you to potential breaches, enabling you to respond promptly and mitigate any potential damage.

Employee training is crucial in maintaining strong cybersecurity. Educate your employees on best practices such as creating strong passwords, recognizing phishing attempts, and securely handling sensitive data. Establish clear protocols for reporting and responding to security incidents, and conduct regular training sessions to reinforce cybersecurity awareness.

Responding promptly to suspected or actual cyber threats or fraud incidents is vital. Develop an incident response plan that outlines the steps to take in the event of a security breach. This plan should include procedures for investigating and containing the incident, notifying affected parties, preserving evidence, and restoring normal operations. Engage with cybersecurity professionals or a dedicated incident response team to ensure a swift and effective response.

Regularly review and update your cybersecurity measures to stay ahead of evolving threats. Stay informed about the latest trends and vulnerabilities in cybersecurity, and consider engaging with external security experts to conduct regular assessments and penetration testing. They can identify vulnerabilities in your systems and provide recommendations for further strengthening your cybersecurity defenses.

By implementing firewalls, antivirus software, and intrusion detection systems, training employees on data security best practices, and promptly responding to security incidents, you can establish a robust cybersecurity posture for your online business. Prioritizing cybersecurity protects your business and customer information, safeguarding your reputation and maintaining trust with your customers.

Resolving domain name and online trademark issues:

When selecting a domain name for your online presence, it is crucial to conduct comprehensive research to avoid trademark infringement and potential conflicts. Start by conducting a thorough search to ensure that your chosen domain name does not infringe upon existing trademarks or violate the intellectual property rights of others. Research trademark databases, domain name registries, and perform online searches to identify any potential conflicts.

Once you have identified a domain name that is clear of trademark conflicts, register it with a reputable domain name provider or registrar. Choose a provider that is known for reliable services, security measures, and customer support. Registering your domain name with a reputable provider helps ensure the proper management and control of your online presence.

In the event of a domain name dispute, familiarize yourself with the domain name dispute resolution processes available. The Uniform Domain-Name Dispute-Resolution Policy (UDRP) is a widely recognized mechanism for resolving disputes related to domain names. Other dispute resolution options may be available depending on the top-level domain (TLD) of your domain name. Familiarize yourself with the specific dispute resolution procedures for your domain name extension and understand the criteria for filing a complaint or defending against one.

To protect your online brand and trademarks effectively, consider consulting with intellectual property attorneys who specialize in domain name disputes and online brand protection. They can provide guidance on registering and protecting your trademarks, navigating dispute resolution processes, and enforcing your rights in the online space.

By conducting thorough research, registering your domain name with a reputable provider, understanding domain name dispute resolution processes, and seeking legal guidance when needed, you can protect your online brand and trademarks and mitigate the risk of disputes or infringements. Safeguarding your online presence is essential for establishing and maintaining a strong and reputable digital presence.

Understanding online advertising and affiliate marketing:

When conducting online advertising for your business, it is crucial to comply with advertising regulations and guidelines, particularly those set forth by the Federal Trade Commission (FTC). Adhering to these regulations helps maintain transparency and consumer trust, while also ensuring compliance with legal requirements.

First and foremost, ensure that your online advertisements are truthful and not deceptive. Clearly and accurately represent your products or services, avoiding any false or misleading claims. Provide clear and substantiated information to consumers, allowing them to make informed decisions about your offerings.

Another important aspect of online advertising compliance is the proper disclosure of advertising content. Ensure that your advertisements are clearly distinguishable from non-advertising content, such as editorial or user-generated content. Clearly label or identify your ads as such to prevent any confusion or deception among consumers.

If you engage in affiliate marketing or have material connections with endorsers or influencers, it is essential to disclose these relationships to consumers. Disclosures help maintain transparency and prevent any potential misleading or deceptive practices. Adhere to the FTC guidelines for disclosures, ensuring that they are clear, conspicuous, and readily understandable to consumers.

Regularly review and stay updated on advertising regulations and guidelines, as they may evolve over time. The FTC provides valuable resources and guidance on advertising compliance, including its Guides Concerning the Use of Endorsements and Testimonials in Advertising. Familiarize yourself with these guidelines to ensure your advertising practices align with legal requirements.

In summary, compliance with advertising regulations and guidelines, particularly those set by the FTC, is crucial for maintaining transparency, consumer trust, and legal compliance in your online advertising efforts. By providing truthful and clear advertisements, properly disclosing advertising content, and adhering to FTC guidelines, you can establish a reputable and compliant online advertising presence for your business.

Expanding into e-commerce and international sales:

Expanding into e-commerce and international sales brings additional legal considerations that must be addressed to ensure compliance and smooth operations. It is essential to familiarize yourself with the applicable laws and regulations governing your specific industry and target markets. Here are some key areas to consider:

Tax requirements: Understand the tax obligations associated with selling products or services online, both domestically and internationally. Be aware of sales tax requirements in different states or countries and comply with tax registration, collection, and reporting obligations. Consult with tax professionals to ensure compliance with applicable tax laws.

Customs duties and import/export regulations: If you are involved in importing or exporting goods across international borders, research and comply with customs duties, import/export restrictions, and documentation requirements of the countries involved. Stay updated on trade agreements, tariff schedules, and customs regulations to navigate international trade effectively.

International privacy laws: When handling customer data in international transactions, be aware of data protection and privacy laws in different jurisdictions. Ensure compliance with regulations such as the European Union's General Data Protection Regulation (GDPR) or other country-specific privacy laws that may apply. Implement appropriate data protection measures and obtain necessary consents when collecting and processing customer data.

Country-specific regulations: Each country may have its own regulations and requirements regarding e-commerce, consumer protection, advertising, and labeling. Understand and comply with these country-specific regulations to ensure legal compliance and maintain a positive reputation in international markets.

Consumer protection laws: Be mindful of consumer protection laws that apply to e-commerce transactions, such as regulations on product warranties, returns and refunds, and consumer rights. Comply with these laws to protect your customers and mitigate potential legal risks.

It is crucial to conduct thorough research and seek professional advice, such as consulting with international trade specialists, tax advisors, and legal professionals experienced in international business law. They can provide guidance tailored to your specific circumstances and help navigate the complexities of expanding into e-commerce and international markets.

By understanding and complying with applicable laws and regulations, you can establish a strong legal foundation for your e-commerce operations and international sales, ensuring compliance, protecting your business, and building trust with customers worldwide.

When starting a small business, it's important to establish a strong online presence to reach a wider audience and maximize your potential for success. Building an effective website is a crucial step in this process. Your website serves as a digital storefront, allowing customers to learn about your products or services, make purchases, and engage with your brand.

When designing your website, it's important to prioritize user experience (UX) and ensure that it is easy to navigate, visually appealing, and optimized for mobile devices. A well-designed website not only attracts and retains visitors but also helps build trust and credibility for your business.

In addition to the design, you should also focus on creating high-quality, informative, and engaging content. This includes product descriptions, blog posts, articles, and other relevant information that showcases your expertise and provides value to your audience. Well-written and optimized content can also improve your search engine rankings, making it easier for potential customers to find your website.

To drive traffic to your website, it's essential to implement effective digital marketing strategies. This may include search engine optimization (SEO) to improve your website's visibility in search engine results, pay-per-click (PPC) advertising campaigns to target specific keywords and demographics, and social media marketing to engage with your target audience.

When conducting digital marketing campaigns, it's important to track and analyze the performance of your efforts. This involves monitoring key metrics such as website traffic, conversion rates, and engagement levels. By analyzing this data, you can make informed decisions to optimize your marketing strategies and improve your return on investment.

As your business grows, it's crucial to prioritize cybersecurity and protect your website and customer data from cyber threats. Implementing robust security measures, such as SSL certificates, firewalls, and regular software updates, can help safeguard your website and provide peace of mind to your customers.

Another important consideration in online business is the legal aspect. Ensure that your website complies with applicable laws and regulations, including privacy laws, consumer protection laws, and intellectual property rights. Display clear terms of service, privacy policies, and disclaimers to inform visitors of their rights and responsibilities.

Incorporating customer feedback mechanisms, such as customer reviews and ratings, can help build trust and credibility. Positive reviews can attract new customers and enhance your reputation, while negative feedback provides an opportunity to address issues and improve your products or services.

Finally, establishing a strong online presence requires ongoing efforts and adaptation. Stay up to date with industry trends, technology advancements, and changes in consumer behavior. Continuously evaluate and refine your online strategies to stay ahead of the competition and meet the evolving needs of your target audience.

By building a compelling website, implementing effective digital marketing strategies, prioritizing cybersecurity, complying with legal requirements, and adapting to market dynamics, you can establish a strong online presence for your small business and increase your chances of long-term success.

Chapter 9:

Commercial Leases and Real Estate

Commercial leases and real estate play a vital role in the success of many small businesses. Understanding the intricacies of commercial leases, real estate transactions, and related legal considerations is essential. This chapter explores key aspects of commercial leases and real estate for small business owners.

Understanding commercial lease agreements:

When entering into a commercial lease agreement, it is crucial to thoroughly understand and negotiate the terms and conditions to protect your business's interests. The lease agreement serves as a legally binding contract between the tenant (your business) and the landlord or property owner.

Key components of a commercial lease agreement include the lease term, which specifies the duration of the lease, whether it is a fixed term or a month-to-month agreement. It is important to consider the length of the lease in relation to your business's needs and growth projections.

The rent structure is another crucial aspect to consider. This includes the base rent, any additional charges such as common area maintenance (CAM) fees or utilities, and the payment schedule. Negotiating favorable rent terms is essential to ensure that the rental costs align with your budget and financial capabilities.

Maintenance responsibilities should be clearly outlined in the lease agreement. This includes defining who is responsible for repairs, maintenance, and any necessary upgrades or improvements. Understanding these obligations can help avoid disputes and ensure that the property is properly maintained.

Permitted uses are restrictions or limitations on how the leased premises can be used. Ensure that the lease agreement allows for your intended business activities and any future expansion plans. It is important to negotiate flexibility in case you need to make changes to your business operations.

The lease agreement should also address renewal options, rent escalations, and potential termination clauses. Renewal options provide you with the opportunity to extend the lease term if desired, while rent escalations may specify how and when the rent will increase over time. Termination clauses outline the conditions under which either party can terminate the lease early.

Assignment and subletting provisions determine whether you have the ability to transfer the lease to another party or sublet the premises to a third party. These provisions can be important if your business needs change or if you wish to exit the lease before the term expires.

Other important considerations in a commercial lease agreement include insurance requirements, indemnification clauses, dispute resolution mechanisms, and any special considerations or concessions negotiated during the lease negotiation process.

It is highly recommended to engage the services of a qualified real estate attorney to review and advise on the lease agreement. An attorney can ensure that the terms are fair and reasonable, protect your interests, and provide guidance on any legal implications.

Taking the time to carefully review and negotiate the terms of a commercial lease agreement is essential to protect your business and establish a positive and mutually beneficial relationship with the landlord.

Negotiating favorable lease terms and conditions:

During lease negotiations, it is important to clearly communicate your business's requirements and objectives. Identify areas where you may have leverage, such as desirable locations, market conditions, or the landlord's need to fill vacancies. Use this leverage to negotiate terms that are favorable to your business.

Negotiating rent amounts involves understanding the market rates for similar properties in the area. Research comparable rental prices and use that information to support your proposed rent. Consider factors such as the length of the lease, the condition of the property, and any unique features or amenities offered.

Lease duration is another negotiation point. Depending on your business's needs and growth projections, you may seek a shorter or longer lease term. A longer-term lease can provide stability, while a shorter-term lease offers flexibility. Evaluate your business's future plans and negotiate a term that aligns with your goals.

Renewal options are important for securing the ability to extend the lease beyond the initial term. Consider negotiating multiple renewal options, each with predetermined rent increases or escalations. This can provide certainty and continuity for your business.

Maintenance responsibilities should be negotiated to ensure fairness and cost efficiency. Determine the extent of your business's obligations and clarify the landlord's responsibilities. Consider negotiating provisions for regular maintenance, repairs, and upgrades, as well as who will be responsible for associated costs.

If desired, negotiate the inclusion of tenant improvement allowances or concessions. This can provide financial assistance for customizing or improving the leased space to meet your specific business needs. Clearly outline the scope and limitations of any improvements or modifications in the lease agreement.

Consulting with a commercial real estate attorney during lease negotiations is highly recommended. An attorney can provide guidance on lease provisions, help identify potential risks, and ensure that the final agreement protects your business's interests. They can also assist in resolving any disputes or issues that may arise during the negotiation process.

Remember that lease negotiations are a give-and-take process. Be prepared to make concessions where necessary, but also advocate for terms that are in the best interest of your business. Taking a proactive and informed approach to lease negotiations can help you secure a lease agreement that meets your needs and supports the success of your business.

Complying with zoning and land use regulations:

Before committing to a commercial lease, it is crucial to thoroughly understand the zoning and land use regulations in the area where the property is located. Zoning laws determine how land can be used and what types of activities are permitted in specific areas. Familiarize yourself with the zoning classification of the property and ensure it aligns with your business activities.

Research the local zoning ordinances and regulations to determine if your intended use is allowed in the designated zone. Some areas may have specific zoning restrictions or require conditional use permits for certain business types. It is essential to comply with these regulations to avoid potential legal issues and disruptions to your business operations.

In addition to zoning regulations, identify any specific permits or licenses required for your business activities. This may include health permits, liquor licenses, signage permits, or other industry-specific authorizations. Research the requirements and application processes for these permits to ensure compliance with local laws and regulations.

Consult with local authorities, such as zoning departments or planning commissions, to clarify any questions or concerns regarding zoning or permit requirements. They can provide guidance and information on the specific regulations that apply to your business and the property you are considering.

Engaging the services of a real estate attorney or a knowledgeable real estate agent can also be beneficial. They can help you navigate the complexities of zoning and land use regulations, review lease agreements for potential issues, and ensure that your business activities are in compliance with local laws.

By conducting thorough research and understanding the zoning and land use regulations, you can make informed decisions when selecting a commercial lease and ensure that your business operations are conducted in accordance with the applicable laws and regulations.

Handling lease renewals, extensions, and terminations:

Lease renewals, extensions, and potential terminations are important considerations when entering into a commercial lease. It is essential to understand the procedures and timeframes outlined in your lease agreement to effectively plan for the future of your business.

Review your lease agreement carefully to determine the specific provisions related to lease renewals and extensions. Note any notice periods or requirements for initiating the renewal or extension process. It is important to adhere to these timelines to ensure you have the opportunity to negotiate favorable terms and avoid any potential automatic lease terminations.

Open communication with your landlord is key. Well in advance of the lease expiration, engage in discussions with your landlord to express your intent to renew or extend the lease. This allows both parties to negotiate terms, such as rental rates, lease duration, and any necessary modifications to the lease agreement. It is beneficial to document any agreed-upon changes in writing and have them incorporated into an amended lease agreement.

If lease renewal or extension is not possible or desired, it is important to understand the procedures for lease termination as outlined in your agreement. This may include notice periods or penalties for early termination. Compliance with these procedures is crucial to avoid potential legal disputes or financial liabilities.

Consider your business's future needs and growth plans when assessing lease renewal or extension options. If your business has outgrown the current space or requires a different location, it may be necessary to explore alternative leasing options or negotiate a new lease agreement elsewhere.

Engaging the services of a real estate attorney can provide valuable guidance and ensure that you fully understand the lease renewal, extension, or termination process. They can help review the lease agreement, advise on negotiation strategies, and protect your interests throughout the process.

By planning ahead, maintaining open communication with your landlord, and seeking professional advice when necessary, you can effectively navigate lease renewals, extensions, or potential terminations and secure the best outcome for your business.

Resolving lease disputes and landlord-tenant issues:

Lease disputes or issues with the landlord can sometimes arise during the course of a commercial lease. It is important to address these matters promptly and seek resolution through appropriate means to protect your business interests.

Open and constructive communication is key when attempting to resolve lease disputes. Start by discussing the issue with your landlord and try to find a mutually acceptable solution through negotiation. Clearly communicate your concerns and desired outcomes, and be willing to listen to the landlord's perspective. Document all discussions and agreements in writing to ensure clarity and avoid any misunderstandings.

If direct negotiations prove challenging or unsuccessful, alternative dispute resolution methods such as mediation or arbitration can be pursued. Mediation involves a neutral third party who facilitates negotiations between the parties to reach a resolution. Arbitration, on the other hand, involves presenting the dispute to a neutral arbitrator who makes a binding decision. These methods can often be faster, less formal, and more cost-effective than litigation.

Consulting with an attorney experienced in commercial lease disputes can provide valuable guidance and representation throughout the dispute resolution process. They can assess the merits of your case, advise on negotiation strategies, and help protect your rights and interests. If litigation becomes necessary, an attorney can represent you in court and advocate for your position.

It is important to maintain detailed records of all lease-related interactions and issues. This includes written correspondence, emails, photographs, and any relevant documentation. These records can serve as evidence if a dispute escalates and can help support your claims or defenses.

Remember that each lease agreement may contain specific provisions regarding dispute resolution. Carefully review your lease agreement to understand any requirements or procedures that must be followed when resolving disputes.

By taking a proactive approach, seeking resolution through negotiation or alternative dispute resolution methods, and consulting with an attorney when needed, you can effectively address lease disputes and protect your business interests.

Considerations for buying or selling commercial property:

When buying or selling commercial property, conducting comprehensive due diligence is crucial to minimize risks and make informed decisions. Start by assessing the physical condition of the property, including its structure, systems, and potential environmental issues. Engage professionals such as inspectors, engineers, and environmental consultants to thoroughly evaluate the property and provide detailed reports.

Reviewing title and survey documents is essential to understand the legal ownership and boundaries of the property. Examine the title history to ensure there are no encumbrances, liens, or disputes that could impact the transaction. Obtain a current survey to verify the property boundaries and identify any potential encroachments or easements.

Environmental considerations are also important, especially if the property has a history of hazardous materials or is located in an environmentally sensitive area. Engage environmental consultants to conduct assessments and provide reports on the property's environmental condition and compliance with regulations.

Engaging professionals in the real estate industry is highly recommended throughout the buying or selling process. Real estate agents can assist in finding suitable properties or buyers, negotiate terms, and facilitate the transaction. Appraisers can provide an unbiased valuation of the property to ensure fair pricing. Attorneys specialized in real estate can review and draft contracts, navigate legal complexities, and protect your interests.

Additionally, consult local zoning and land use regulations to ensure the property is suitable for your intended use. Research any permits, licenses, or restrictions that may apply. It is essential to comply with all applicable laws and regulations to avoid legal issues in the future.

Performing thorough due diligence allows you to assess the risks and benefits of the property and make informed decisions. It also provides an opportunity to identify any potential issues or contingencies that may need to be addressed in the purchase or sale agreement.

By engaging professionals, carefully reviewing documents, and conducting comprehensive assessments, you can mitigate risks and ensure a smooth and legally compliant transaction when buying or selling commercial property.

Understanding property insurance and liability issues:

Obtaining the right property insurance coverage is crucial to protect your investment and mitigate potential risks. There are several types of insurance policies to consider when it comes to commercial property:

1. General Liability Insurance: This coverage protects you from third-party claims for bodily injury or property damage that may occur on your property. It provides financial protection in case of lawsuits or legal claims.
2. Property Insurance: Property insurance covers physical damage to your property caused by perils such as fire, theft, vandalism, or natural disasters. It typically includes coverage for the building structure and its contents.

3. Business Interruption Insurance: This type of insurance provides coverage for lost income and additional expenses if your business operations are disrupted due to covered perils, such as a fire or natural disaster. It helps to replace lost revenue and cover ongoing expenses during the interruption period.

It's important to carefully review and understand the terms, coverage limits, deductibles, and exclusions of each insurance policy. Consider consulting with an insurance professional who specializes in commercial property insurance to ensure you have the appropriate coverage for your specific needs.

As a tenant, it's also essential to understand your responsibilities regarding insurance coverage. Review your lease agreement to determine the insurance requirements set by the landlord, such as the types and minimum coverage limits. Make sure you comply with these requirements and provide proof of insurance as requested.

If you are the property owner, it's important to maintain adequate insurance coverage on the property itself. Additionally, you may want to consider liability insurance to protect yourself against claims from tenants or visitors to the property.

Regularly review and update your insurance coverage as your business and property needs evolve. Periodically reassess your coverage limits to ensure they align with the value of your property and potential risks.

By obtaining the appropriate property insurance coverage, you can protect your investment, mitigate financial risks, and have peace of mind knowing that you are prepared for unexpected events that may occur on or affect your property.

Environmental regulations and compliance:

When it comes to commercial property, it is important to be aware of potential environmental risks and comply with applicable environmental laws and regulations. Here are some key considerations:

1. Environmental Due Diligence: Before purchasing or leasing commercial property, consider conducting a Phase I Environmental Site Assessment (ESA). This assessment helps identify potential environmental risks and liabilities associated with the property. It typically involves a review of historical records, site inspections, and interviews with past and current property owners and occupants.

2. Compliance with Environmental Laws: Familiarize yourself with federal, state, and local environmental laws and regulations that may apply to your property. These may include regulations related to hazardous materials, waste disposal, air quality, water quality, and land use. Ensure compliance with these laws to avoid potential legal issues and penalties.

3. Hazardous Materials: If your business involves the use, storage, or disposal of hazardous materials, understand and comply with applicable regulations. This may include obtaining permits, implementing proper storage and handling practices, and having emergency response plans in place.

4. Waste Management: Properly manage waste generated by your business operations. This includes following appropriate disposal procedures for hazardous and non-hazardous waste, recycling whenever possible, and ensuring compliance with waste management regulations.

5. Pollution Prevention: Implement measures to prevent pollution and minimize your environmental footprint. This may include energy conservation practices, reducing water usage, using environmentally friendly materials and products, and implementing sustainable practices.

6. Environmental Liability: Be aware of potential environmental liabilities associated with your property. This could include contamination from previous activities or operations on the property. Consider obtaining appropriate insurance coverage, such as pollution liability insurance, to protect against potential environmental claims or cleanup costs.

7. Consult with Environmental Professionals: If you have concerns about environmental issues related to your commercial property, it may be beneficial to consult with environmental professionals, such as environmental consultants or attorneys with expertise in environmental law. They can provide guidance, conduct assessments, and help ensure compliance with environmental regulations.

By being proactive in addressing environmental considerations, you can minimize risks, protect the environment, and maintain compliance with applicable laws and regulations. This not only helps safeguard your business but also demonstrates your commitment to environmental responsibility.

By understanding commercial lease agreements, negotiating favorable terms, complying with regulations, and addressing real estate-related issues, you can effectively manage your business's real estate needs. Seek guidance from legal professionals experienced in commercial leases and real estate to ensure compliance, protect your interests, and minimize legal risks.

Chapter 10:

Taxation for Small Businesses

Understanding and managing tax obligations is an essential aspect of running a small business. This chapter provides guidance on key tax considerations for small business owners, ensuring compliance and optimizing tax strategies.

Understanding federal and state tax obligations:

When it comes to taxes, it is crucial to familiarize yourself with both federal and state tax obligations. Here are some key considerations:

1. Federal Taxes: Understand your federal tax obligations, including income tax, self-employment tax (if applicable), and employment taxes if you have employees. Consult the Internal Revenue Service (IRS) guidelines and publications to determine your filing requirements, deadlines, and any deductions or credits you may be eligible for.
2. State Taxes: Research the specific state tax requirements in the state where your business is located or operates. This may include state income tax, sales tax, and employer taxes such as unemployment insurance and disability insurance. Check with your state's Department of Revenue or Taxation for guidance on filing requirements, tax rates, and any state-specific deductions or credits.
3. Filing and Payment Deadlines: Understand the deadlines for filing your federal and state tax returns, as well as making tax payments. These deadlines can vary depending on your business structure and tax year. It is important to meet these deadlines to avoid penalties and interest charges.
4. Record-Keeping: Maintain organized and accurate financial records, including income, expenses, and supporting documentation. Good record-keeping is essential for preparing and filing your tax returns, as well as for substantiating deductions and credits claimed.
5. Tax Deductions and Credits: Familiarize yourself with the tax deductions and credits available to your business. These can help reduce your taxable income and lower your overall tax liability. Common deductions include business expenses, depreciation of assets, and health insurance premiums. Tax credits may be available for certain activities such as research

and development, hiring certain employees, or investing in renewable energy.

6. Quarterly Estimated Taxes: If your business has income that is not subject to withholding taxes, such as self-employment income or rental income, you may need to make quarterly estimated tax payments to the IRS and state tax authorities. Calculate your estimated tax liability and make timely payments to avoid underpayment penalties.

7. Sales Tax Collection and Reporting: If your business sells taxable goods or services, you may be required to collect sales tax from customers and remit it to the appropriate state tax authority. Understand the sales tax regulations in your state, including registration requirements, filing frequencies, and reporting obligations.

8. Seek Professional Advice: Tax laws can be complex, and it is advisable to seek professional advice from a certified public accountant (CPA) or tax attorney to ensure compliance and maximize tax benefits. They can help you navigate the intricacies of the tax code, answer specific questions related to your business, and assist with tax planning strategies.

9. Stay Informed: Tax laws and regulations are subject to change, so it is important to stay informed about updates and revisions that may impact your business. Regularly review IRS publications, state tax agency websites, and consult with tax professionals to stay up to date with any changes that may affect your tax obligations.

By understanding and fulfilling your federal and state tax obligations, you can ensure compliance, minimize tax liabilities, and avoid penalties or legal issues. Consulting with tax professionals can provide valuable guidance tailored to your specific business circumstances and help optimize your tax strategy.

Choosing the right tax structure for your business:

When choosing a tax structure for your business, it is crucial to consider various factors that can impact your tax obligations, liability protection, and operational requirements. Here are some key points to consider:

1. Sole Proprietorship: This is the simplest form of business structure, where the business is owned and operated by a single individual. As a sole proprietor, you report business income and expenses on your personal tax return (Form 1040)

using Schedule C. While a sole proprietorship offers simplicity and flexibility, it does not provide personal liability protection, and the owner is personally responsible for all business debts and obligations.

2. Partnership: A partnership involves two or more individuals who share ownership and management of the business. Partners report their share of business income and expenses on their personal tax returns using Form 1065. Partnerships do not pay income tax at the entity level, but rather, the profits or losses flow through to the partners' personal tax returns. Partnerships offer flexibility and shared decision-making but do not provide personal liability protection for partners.

3. Corporation: A corporation is a separate legal entity from its owners, known as shareholders. It offers personal liability protection to shareholders, meaning their personal assets are generally not at risk for the corporation's debts or liabilities. Corporations are subject to corporate income tax at the entity level, and shareholders report any dividends or salaries received on their personal tax returns. There are different types of corporations, such as C corporations and S corporations, each with their own tax rules and requirements.

4. Limited Liability Company (LLC): An LLC combines elements of both a corporation and a partnership. It offers personal liability protection to its members (owners) while allowing flexibility in tax treatment. By default, an LLC is taxed as a partnership, with income and expenses flowing through to the members' personal tax returns. However, an LLC can also elect to be taxed as a corporation (C corporation or S corporation) if it meets the eligibility requirements. An LLC provides flexibility in terms of management structure and operational requirements.

When selecting a tax structure, it is essential to consider not only the tax implications but also the legal and operational aspects of your business. Factors such as the nature of your business, the number of owners, the desired level of liability protection, and future growth plans should be taken into account.

Consulting with a tax advisor or attorney who specializes in business taxation can provide valuable insights and help you navigate the complexities of tax laws. They can assess your specific business needs, analyze the potential tax implications of different structures, and guide you in selecting the most suitable tax structure for your business.

Remember that tax considerations should be just one part of your decision-making process. It is also important to evaluate other factors, such as legal protection, operational flexibility, and long-term business goals, when determining the optimal tax structure for your business.

Navigating sales tax requirements and exemptions:

If your business involves selling goods or certain services, it is important to comply with sales tax requirements in your state. Here are some key considerations:

1. Register for a sales tax permit: Most states require businesses to register for a sales tax permit before they can collect and remit sales tax. Contact your state's department of revenue or taxation to understand the registration process and any specific requirements.
2. Determine your sales tax nexus: Sales tax nexus refers to the connection between your business and a state that triggers the obligation to collect and remit sales tax. Nexus can be established through various factors, such as having a physical presence (e.g., office, store, warehouse) in the state, making regular sales to customers in the state, or exceeding certain sales thresholds. Understand the nexus rules in the states where you have a presence or significant sales to determine your sales tax obligations.
3. Collect and remit sales tax: Once you have your sales tax permit, you are responsible for collecting sales tax from your customers at the appropriate rate and remitting it to the state's taxing authority. Sales tax rates can vary depending on the location and type of goods or services sold. Implement systems to accurately calculate and track sales tax and ensure timely remittance to avoid penalties or fines.
4. Understand exemptions and special rules: Some states provide exemptions or reduced tax rates for certain goods, services, or types of businesses. Familiarize yourself with any exemptions or special rules that may apply to your industry or specific transactions. Keep documentation to support any exempt sales or taxable sales subject to a reduced rate.
5. Stay updated on changes: Sales tax laws and regulations can change over time. Stay informed about any updates, new legislation, or changes in rates or exemptions that may impact your sales tax obligations. Regularly review guidance provided

by your state's taxing authority or consult with a tax advisor to ensure compliance.
6. Maintain records: Keep detailed records of your sales transactions, including invoices, receipts, and sales tax returns. These records will be essential for accurate reporting, auditing purposes, and any potential sales tax inquiries or disputes.

It is important to note that sales tax requirements can vary by state, and each state has its own regulations and procedures. Consult with a tax professional or attorney specializing in sales tax to understand the specific requirements and ensure compliance with your state's laws.

Properly managing sales tax obligations not only helps you meet your legal responsibilities but also establishes trust with your customers and avoids potential penalties or legal issues associated with non-compliance.

Deductions and credits available to small businesses:

Familiarizing yourself with tax deductions and credits is an important step in optimizing your tax liability. Here are some key considerations:

1. Business-related expenses: Keep track of all business-related expenses throughout the year, such as office supplies, equipment, advertising costs, travel expenses, and professional services. These expenses are generally deductible and can help lower your taxable income.
2. Home office deduction: If you use a portion of your home exclusively for business purposes, you may be eligible for a home office deduction. This deduction allows you to deduct a portion of your home expenses, such as rent or mortgage interest, utilities, and insurance, based on the percentage of your home used for business.
3. Healthcare-related deductions: Self-employed individuals may be eligible to deduct health insurance premiums, as well as certain medical and dental expenses, for themselves, their spouses, and dependents. Understanding the specific requirements and limitations for these deductions can help reduce your taxable income.
4. Retirement contributions: Contributions to retirement plans, such as Simplified Employee Pension (SEP) IRAs or solo 401(k) plans, can provide tax advantages. These contributions are

typically deductible and can help lower your taxable income while saving for retirement.

5. Research and Development (R&D) credit: If your business engages in qualified research and development activities, you may be eligible for the R&D credit. This credit provides an incentive to encourage innovation and technological advancements and can significantly reduce your tax liability.

6. Small Business Health Care Tax Credit: Small businesses that provide health insurance to their employees may qualify for the Small Business Health Care Tax Credit. This credit can help offset a portion of the costs associated with providing health insurance coverage.

It is important to consult with a qualified tax professional or accountant to understand the specific deductions and credits available to your business. They can help you navigate the complex tax laws, identify eligible deductions, and ensure proper documentation and compliance.

Keep in mind that tax laws and regulations may change, so staying updated on any new developments or legislative changes is crucial. By taking advantage of available deductions and credits, you can lower your tax liability and keep more of your hard-earned money in your business.

Handling payroll taxes and reporting requirements:

If you have employees, it is important to understand and fulfill your payroll tax obligations. Here are some key considerations:

1. Withholding income tax, Social Security, and Medicare: As an employer, you are responsible for withholding the appropriate amounts for federal income tax, Social Security tax, and Medicare tax from your employees' wages. The withholding amounts are based on the information provided by employees on their Form W-4.

2. Accurate record-keeping: Maintain accurate records of employee wages, tax withholdings, and other payroll-related information. This includes keeping track of hours worked, calculating overtime wages if applicable, and maintaining records of any benefits provided.

3. Timely payroll tax deposits: Ensure that you deposit the withheld income tax, Social Security tax, and Medicare tax in a timely manner. The frequency of these deposits depends on

your business's size and can be monthly or semiweekly. Consult the IRS guidelines or a tax professional to determine your deposit schedule.

4. Filing payroll tax returns: File payroll tax returns, such as Form 941 (Employer's Quarterly Federal Tax Return), on time. These returns report the wages paid, the taxes withheld, and the employer's portion of Social Security and Medicare taxes. Additionally, you may need to file state payroll tax returns and other local tax returns, depending on your location.

5. Form W-2 and Form 1099 reporting: Provide Form W-2 to employees by January 31 of each year, which summarizes their annual wages and tax withholdings. If you engage independent contractors, you may need to issue Form 1099-MISC to report payments made to them, if applicable. Ensure that you comply with the reporting requirements and deadlines set by the IRS.

6. Payroll tax deposits and reporting for state and local taxes: In addition to federal payroll taxes, be aware of any state and local payroll tax obligations. Each state and locality may have specific requirements for withholding, reporting, and remitting payroll taxes. Familiarize yourself with the regulations in your jurisdiction and ensure compliance.

Payroll tax compliance can be complex, and it is recommended to work with a qualified payroll service provider or tax professional to ensure accurate calculations, timely filings, and compliance with all applicable laws and regulations. They can assist you in understanding your specific obligations and help navigate any payroll tax-related issues that may arise.

By fulfilling your payroll tax obligations, you not only comply with legal requirements but also ensure that your employees' tax obligations are met and avoid potential penalties or audits. s.

Quarterly and annual tax filing and payment obligations:

To stay compliant with tax obligations, it is crucial to be aware of key tax filing deadlines and pay estimated taxes on time. Here are some important considerations:

1. Quarterly estimated taxes: If you expect to owe a significant amount of tax at the end of the year, you may be required to make quarterly estimated tax payments. These payments typically cover your federal income tax liability, as well as any

applicable state and local taxes. Be sure to understand the estimated tax payment requirements and due dates set by the IRS and your state tax authority. Failure to make timely estimated tax payments may result in penalties and interest.

2. Annual tax return filings: For most businesses, the tax year ends on December 31, and the annual tax return must be filed by the due date. The due date for federal income tax returns for businesses varies depending on the business structure. For example, corporations generally file Form 1120 by the 15th day of the third month after the end of their tax year, while partnerships and S corporations file Form 1065 and Form 1120-S respectively by the 15th day of the third month after the end of the tax year.

3. Organized record-keeping: Maintain organized and accurate records to support your tax filings. This includes keeping track of income, expenses, receipts, invoices, and other relevant financial documentation. Proper record-keeping is essential for substantiating your tax deductions, credits, and any other claims on your tax return. It also helps facilitate the tax preparation process and can be invaluable in the event of an audit or review by tax authorities.

4. Forms and schedules: Understand the specific forms and schedules required for your business type. The IRS provides a wide range of forms and schedules to accommodate different business structures and activities. Ensure that you are using the correct forms and schedules and accurately report the information required. Consulting with a tax professional or utilizing tax preparation software can help ensure the proper completion of your tax forms.

5. Seek professional assistance: Tax laws and regulations can be complex and subject to frequent changes. Consider working with a qualified tax professional, such as a certified public accountant (CPA) or tax attorney, to ensure accurate and compliant tax filings. They can provide guidance on tax planning, identify deductions and credits, help navigate complex tax rules, and ensure that you meet all filing deadlines.

By staying aware of tax filing deadlines, making timely estimated tax payments, maintaining organized records, and seeking professional assistance when needed, you can fulfill your tax obligations and minimize the risk of penalties, interest, or other tax-related issues.

Compliance with tax laws not only helps you avoid legal problems but also ensures that your business operates smoothly and efficiently from a financial perspective.

Record-keeping for tax purposes and IRS audits:

Establishing effective record-keeping practices is essential for supporting your tax filings and potential IRS audits. Here are some key considerations:

1. Organize financial documents: Keep all financial documents in an organized manner. This includes invoices, receipts, bank statements, credit card statements, canceled checks, and any other documents related to income and expenses. Maintain separate files for different types of transactions to facilitate easy retrieval and categorization.
2. Maintain accurate and complete records: Ensure that your records are accurate, complete, and up to date. Double-check entries for accuracy and ensure that all transactions are properly recorded. Include detailed information such as the date, amount, purpose, and parties involved in each transaction.
3. Retain records for the recommended period: The IRS has guidelines on how long you should keep tax-related records. Generally, it is recommended to retain records for at least three to seven years, depending on the type of document and the nature of your business. This includes tax returns, supporting documents, employment tax records, and any other records relevant to your tax filings.
4. Store records securely: Keep your financial records in a safe and secure location to protect them from loss, damage, or unauthorized access. Consider digital storage options, such as cloud-based solutions or encrypted external hard drives, to ensure backup and easy access to your records.
5. Segregate personal and business expenses: Maintain a clear separation between personal and business expenses. Use separate bank accounts and credit cards for business transactions to simplify record-keeping and avoid any potential confusion or complications.
6. Use accounting software: Consider using accounting software to streamline your record-keeping process. Accounting software can help automate data entry, generate financial reports, and

provide a centralized system for managing your financial records. Choose software that is suitable for your business size and needs.

7. Seek professional guidance: If you are uncertain about record-keeping requirements or need assistance in setting up an effective system, consult with a tax professional or an accountant. They can provide guidance specific to your business and help ensure compliance with record-keeping rules and regulations.

8. Be prepared for audits: In the event of an IRS audit, having well-organized and comprehensive records will help you respond to inquiries and substantiate the information reported on your tax returns. Familiarize yourself with the IRS audit process and understand your rights and responsibilities. If you receive an audit notice, consult with a tax professional to guide you through the audit process.

By establishing effective record-keeping practices, you can accurately report your income and expenses, support your tax filings, and be prepared for potential IRS audits. Good record-keeping not only ensures compliance with tax laws but also provides valuable insights into your business's financial health and helps you make informed decisions.

Engaging with tax professionals and staying updated on tax laws:

Engaging with tax professionals is highly recommended to ensure accurate tax planning and compliance for your business. Here are some key considerations:

1. Certified public accountants (CPAs): CPAs are qualified professionals who specialize in accounting and taxation. They can assist with tax planning, preparation, and compliance. CPAs have extensive knowledge of tax laws and regulations and can provide valuable insights tailored to your business's specific needs.

2. Tax attorneys: Tax attorneys specialize in tax law and can provide legal advice and guidance on complex tax matters. They can help you navigate intricate tax issues, interpret tax laws, and represent your interests in case of disputes or audits.

3. Proactive tax planning: Work with tax professionals to develop proactive tax planning strategies. They can help you identify deductions, credits, and other tax-saving opportunities specific

to your business. By planning ahead, you can optimize your tax position and minimize your tax liability.

4. Stay updated on tax laws and changes: Tax laws and regulations are subject to regular updates and changes. It's important to stay informed to ensure compliance. Attend tax seminars, workshops, or webinars offered by reputable organizations to keep abreast of the latest developments. Consult reliable tax publications and utilize online resources provided by tax authorities to stay updated on tax laws and changes relevant to your business.

5. Seek guidance for specific situations: Tax professionals can provide guidance for specific situations that may have unique tax implications. Whether it's expanding your business, acquiring assets, engaging in international transactions, or any other significant business event, consult with tax professionals to understand the tax implications and ensure compliance.

6. Addressing IRS audits or disputes: If you encounter an IRS audit or dispute, tax professionals can provide valuable assistance. They can help you respond to inquiries, gather and present supporting documentation, and represent your interests during the audit or dispute resolution process.

7. Collaboration with other professionals: Tax professionals often work closely with other professionals, such as attorneys, financial advisors, and business consultants. Collaborating with a team of professionals can provide comprehensive guidance and ensure that all aspects of your business are considered in the tax planning process.

8. Ethics and confidentiality: When working with tax professionals, ensure that they adhere to professional ethics and maintain client confidentiality. Discuss the scope of their services, fees, and any confidentiality agreements before engaging their services.

By engaging with tax professionals, staying updated on tax laws, and proactively planning for your tax obligations, you can navigate the complexities of taxation with confidence. Working with experts in the field will help ensure accurate tax compliance and optimize your business's financial position.

By understanding and managing your tax obligations effectively, you can optimize tax strategies, ensure compliance, and minimize the risk of penalties or audits. Consult with tax professionals to navigate complex tax matters, develop tax planning strategies, and stay updated on changes in tax laws that may impact your business.

Tax professionals, such as certified public accountants (CPAs) or tax attorneys, have the expertise and knowledge to assist you in various aspects of taxation. They can help you with tax planning, preparation, and compliance, taking into account the specific needs and circumstances of your business. They can guide you in identifying potential deductions, credits, and tax-saving opportunities, maximizing your tax benefits while staying within the boundaries of tax laws and regulations.

Staying updated on tax laws and regulations is crucial, as tax laws can change periodically. Tax professionals can help you stay informed about new developments and ensure that your business remains in compliance with the latest tax requirements. They can provide insights into the specific tax obligations applicable to your industry or business activities and help you address any unique tax situations that may arise.

Effective record-keeping is essential for supporting your tax filings and potential audits. Tax professionals can guide you on best practices for record-keeping, ensuring that you maintain accurate and organized records of your income, expenses, receipts, invoices, and other relevant financial documents. They can advise you on how long to retain these records and what documentation is necessary to substantiate your tax filings.

In the event of an IRS audit or dispute, tax professionals can provide valuable assistance. They can help you navigate the audit process, respond to IRS inquiries, and represent your interests. Their expertise and knowledge of tax laws and regulations can be instrumental in ensuring a favorable outcome and minimizing the impact on your business.

Collaborating with tax professionals allows you to focus on your core business operations while having the peace of mind that your tax obligations are being handled by experts. They can help you proactively plan for your tax obligations, optimize your tax position, and provide guidance on complex tax matters. Additionally, they can assist in addressing any tax-related concerns or questions that may arise, providing you with comprehensive support and expertise.

Chapter 11

Business Insurance and Risk Management

Business insurance is crucial for protecting your small business from unexpected events and potential liabilities. This chapter explores key considerations in assessing insurance needs, understanding different types of coverage, and implementing effective risk management strategies.

Assessing the insurance needs of your business:

Evaluate the unique risks associated with your business operations, industry, and location. Consider potential liabilities, property damage, business interruption, and employee-related risks. Conduct a comprehensive risk assessment to identify the types and levels of coverage required.

Each business has its own set of risks and vulnerabilities. It is essential to assess and understand these risks to adequately protect your business from potential financial losses. Start by identifying the specific risks that your business may face. These can include liabilities arising from product or service defects, accidents or injuries on your premises, professional errors or negligence, data breaches or cyber-attacks, natural disasters, and other unforeseen events that could disrupt your operations.

Consider the nature of your industry and the specific risks associated with it. Certain industries, such as construction, healthcare, or manufacturing, may have higher levels of inherent risks. Take into account any regulatory requirements or industry-specific risks that you must address.

Location can also impact your risk profile. Evaluate factors such as the local climate, crime rates, proximity to hazardous materials, and the stability of the area. These factors can affect the likelihood and severity of certain risks, such as property damage from natural disasters or theft.

Once you have identified the risks, determine the appropriate insurance coverage to mitigate those risks. Common types of business insurance include general liability insurance, property insurance, professional liability insurance (also known as errors and omissions insurance), cyber liability insurance, business interruption insurance, and workers' compensation insurance.

General liability insurance protects your business against third-party claims for bodily injury, property damage, or personal injury. Property insurance covers physical assets, such as buildings, equipment, and inventory, against damage or loss due to fire, theft, or other covered perils. Professional liability insurance is essential for businesses that provide professional services and protects against claims of negligence, errors, or omissions.

Cyber liability insurance helps protect your business against the financial losses and legal liabilities associated with data breaches and cyber-attacks. Business interruption insurance provides coverage for lost income and additional expenses incurred when your business is unable to operate due to a covered event, such as a fire or natural disaster. Workers' compensation insurance is typically required if you have employees and covers medical expenses and lost wages in the event of work-related injuries or illnesses.

Work with an insurance professional who understands your industry and can help tailor insurance coverage to meet your specific needs. They can assist you in determining appropriate coverage limits, deductibles, and policy terms that align with your risk profile and budget.

Regularly review your insurance coverage as your business evolves and new risks emerge. Communicate with your insurance provider to ensure that your coverage remains up to date and sufficient to protect your business adequately. By conducting a comprehensive risk assessment and obtaining the appropriate insurance coverage, you can minimize potential financial losses and safeguard the continuity of your business.

Understanding different types of business insurance:

Familiarize yourself with various types of business insurance to protect your business from a range of potential risks. Here are some examples of commonly used insurance policies:

1. General liability insurance: This coverage protects your business against claims of bodily injury, property damage, or personal injury caused by your business operations, products, or services. It helps cover legal costs and settlements if you are sued.
2. Professional liability insurance (errors and omissions insurance): This type of insurance is essential for businesses that provide professional services or advice. It protects against claims of

negligence, errors, or omissions that may result in financial losses for clients.

3. Property insurance: Property insurance covers physical assets, such as buildings, equipment, inventory, and furniture, against damage or loss caused by events like fire, theft, vandalism, or natural disasters.

4. Workers' compensation insurance: If you have employees, workers' compensation insurance is typically required by law. It provides coverage for medical expenses and lost wages for employees who suffer work-related injuries or illnesses.

5. Business interruption insurance: This coverage helps protect your business from financial losses due to an interruption in operations caused by covered events, such as fire, natural disasters, or other unforeseen circumstances. It can compensate for lost income and help cover ongoing expenses during the recovery period.

6. Cybersecurity insurance: In today's digital landscape, cybersecurity insurance is becoming increasingly important. It provides protection against financial losses and liabilities resulting from data breaches, cyber-attacks, or other cyber incidents.

Assess which types of coverage are relevant for your business based on your industry, size, and specific risks. Consult with an insurance professional or broker who specializes in business insurance to evaluate your needs and customize coverage that aligns with your risk profile. They can help determine appropriate coverage limits, deductibles, and policy terms.

Keep in mind that insurance needs may evolve as your business grows or changes. Regularly review your insurance policies to ensure they remain adequate and up to date. Working closely with an insurance professional will help you make informed decisions to protect your business from various risks and potential liabilities.

Liability insurance and protection from lawsuits:

Obtaining general liability insurance is crucial for businesses to protect against claims of bodily injury, property damage, or personal injury. This type of insurance provides coverage for legal expenses and potential damages resulting from lawsuits filed by third parties. It helps protect your business assets and provides financial support to handle the costs associated with legal defense, settlement, or judgment.

Professional liability insurance, also known as errors and omissions insurance, is particularly important for businesses that provide services or professional advice. This coverage protects against claims of negligence, errors, or omissions that may result in financial losses for clients. Professional liability insurance can cover legal expenses, settlements, or judgments related to professional negligence claims.

The specific coverage and limits of general liability and professional liability insurance can vary depending on the nature of your business, industry, and risk factors. It is important to carefully review policy terms, coverage exclusions, and limitations to ensure that the insurance meets your specific needs.

Consulting with an insurance professional or broker who specializes in business insurance can help you determine the appropriate coverage amounts and policy terms based on your specific business activities and risks. They can assess your unique circumstances and guide you in selecting the right insurance policies to protect your business from potential liabilities and legal claims.

Remember, having the appropriate insurance coverage in place can provide peace of mind and financial protection, allowing you to focus on running your business with confidence.

Property insurance for physical assets and equipment:

Property insurance is a critical component of risk management for businesses, as it protects against losses or damages to physical assets. This type of insurance covers a wide range of property, including buildings, equipment, inventory, supplies, and other tangible assets that are essential to your business operations.

Property insurance provides financial protection in the event of various perils, such as natural disasters (e.g., hurricanes, earthquakes), fire, theft, vandalism, and other covered risks. It can help cover the costs of repairing or replacing damaged property, minimizing the financial impact on your business.

When selecting property insurance coverage, it is important to assess the specific risks associated with your business location and industry. Consider factors such as the geographical region, climate, susceptibility to natural disasters, and the value of your assets. Your coverage should adequately protect against these risks and ensure that the policy limits are sufficient to cover potential losses.

Working with an insurance professional who specializes in commercial property insurance can help you identify the appropriate coverage options for your business. They can assess your specific needs, help determine the value of your assets, and recommend coverage limits that align with your risk profile.

Regularly review and update your property insurance policy as your business grows and changes. This ensures that your coverage remains adequate and up to date with any expansions, acquisitions, or changes in asset values.

Remember, property insurance is an important safeguard for your business, providing financial protection and helping you recover from unforeseen events that could otherwise have a significant impact on your operations.

Workers' compensation and employee injury coverage:

Workers' compensation insurance is a vital component of business insurance, particularly for employers with employees. It is designed to provide coverage for medical expenses, rehabilitation costs, and lost wages for employees who are injured or become ill as a result of their work.

In most states, workers' compensation insurance is mandatory for businesses that have employees. The specific requirements and regulations vary by state, so it is crucial to understand and comply with the laws in your jurisdiction.

Workers' compensation insurance serves as a safety net for both employees and employers. It helps injured or ill workers receive the necessary medical treatment and compensation for lost wages, while also protecting employers from potential lawsuits and financial liabilities arising from workplace injuries or illnesses.

When obtaining workers' compensation insurance, it is important to work with a reputable insurance provider who understands the specific requirements and regulations in your state. They can help you navigate the process, ensure compliance, and tailor coverage to meet the needs of your business.

To ensure proper coverage, accurately report your employee count, job classifications, and payroll information to the insurance provider. This information is used to determine the appropriate premium and coverage limits.

In the event of a workplace injury or illness, promptly report the incident to your insurance carrier. Compliance with reporting procedures is crucial for the timely processing of claims and to ensure that injured employees receive the necessary benefits and support.

By maintaining workers' compensation insurance, you demonstrate your commitment to the well-being and safety of your employees. It provides peace of mind for both you and your workforce, ensuring that they are protected in the event of a workplace accident or illness.

Business interruption insurance and contingency planning:

Business interruption insurance is a valuable coverage that helps businesses recover financially from unforeseen events or disruptions that result in the interruption of their operations. This type of insurance provides coverage for lost income and extra expenses incurred during the period of interruption.

Business interruption insurance is typically triggered by events such as natural disasters (e.g., fires, floods, earthquakes), equipment breakdowns, or other unforeseen circumstances that render the business temporarily unable to operate. It compensates the business for the income it would have earned during the period of interruption, allowing the business to meet its financial obligations, pay its employees, and cover ongoing expenses.

When obtaining business interruption insurance, it is important to carefully review the policy terms, coverage limits, and exclusions. Understand the specific events or perils covered, as well as the waiting period before coverage kicks in. Work closely with an insurance professional to assess the risks faced by your business and select appropriate coverage limits to ensure that your financial losses are adequately covered.

Developing a comprehensive contingency plan is also crucial for business continuity during disruptions. Identify critical business functions and develop strategies to minimize the impact of potential disruptions. This may include implementing backup systems, establishing alternative work locations, and ensuring data backups and recovery plans are in place.

Regularly review and update your contingency plan to account for changes in your business operations, technology, and potential risks. By having a well-thought-out plan in place, you can mitigate the impact of disruptions and facilitate a quicker recovery.

Business interruption insurance is a valuable tool to protect your business's financial stability and ensure its ability to recover from unexpected events. By combining this coverage with a robust contingency plan, you can minimize the impact of interruptions and maintain business continuity.

Managing risk and implementing risk mitigation strategies:

Identifying potential risks and implementing strategies to mitigate them is a critical aspect of risk management for businesses. By proactively addressing risks, businesses can minimize the likelihood and impact of negative events. Here are some key areas to consider:

1. Physical Risks: Assess potential physical risks in your business environment, such as accidents, natural disasters, or security breaches. Implement safety protocols, provide adequate training to employees, and maintain equipment and facilities to minimize the risk of injuries or property damage. Regular inspections and maintenance can help identify and address potential hazards.

2. Cybersecurity Risks: In today's digital landscape, businesses face cybersecurity threats such as data breaches, hacking, and ransomware attacks. Implement robust data protection measures, including firewalls, secure networks, and encryption. Regularly update software and systems to address vulnerabilities and educate employees on cybersecurity best practices, such as strong password management and recognizing phishing attempts.

3. Financial Risks: Assess financial risks, such as cash flow fluctuations, economic downturns, or changes in market conditions. Develop financial contingency plans, maintain a robust cash flow management system, and diversify revenue sources to mitigate the impact of potential financial challenges. Consider appropriate insurance coverage, such as business interruption insurance, to protect against financial losses.

4. Legal and Compliance Risks: Stay informed about legal and regulatory requirements relevant to your business. Develop policies and procedures to ensure compliance with laws and regulations, such as labor laws, data privacy regulations, and

industry-specific regulations. Regularly review and update these policies to adapt to changing legal requirements.

5. Reputation Risks: Safeguard your business's reputation by providing quality products or services and delivering excellent customer service. Implement effective communication strategies to manage potential crises or negative publicity. Monitor online reviews and feedback to address customer concerns promptly and maintain a positive brand image.

6. Supply Chain Risks: Assess risks related to your supply chain, such as disruptions in the availability of raw materials or reliance on a single supplier. Diversify suppliers, maintain good relationships with key partners, and consider contingency plans for alternative sourcing options in case of supply chain disruptions.

7. Employee Risks: Address risks related to your employees, such as workplace injuries, discrimination claims, or employee misconduct. Implement proper training programs, establish clear policies and procedures, and ensure compliance with labor laws and regulations. Maintain a safe and inclusive work environment to minimize the risk of legal issues and employee dissatisfaction.

Regularly review and reassess your risk management strategies to adapt to changing circumstances, industry trends, and emerging risks. Seek input from employees, industry experts, and legal professionals to ensure a comprehensive and effective risk management approach for your business.

Evaluating insurance policies and working with insurance agents:

When purchasing insurance coverage for your business, it is crucial to review policies carefully to ensure you have the right coverage for your specific needs. Here are some important considerations:

1. Policy Terms and Conditions: Read and understand the terms and conditions of the insurance policy. Pay attention to key details such as the coverage period, renewal terms, cancellation policy, and any limitations or restrictions that may apply.

2. Coverage Types and Limits: Determine the types of coverage you need based on your business's specific risks and requirements. Examples include general liability insurance, professional liability insurance, property insurance, workers' compensation insurance, and cyber liability insurance. Assess

the coverage limits to ensure they adequately protect your business in the event of a claim.

3. Exclusions and Deductibles: Take note of any exclusions in the policy that may limit or exclude coverage for certain types of risks or events. Understand the deductibles that apply, which is the amount you must pay out of pocket before the insurance coverage kicks in. Consider whether the deductibles are affordable for your business.

4. Additional Coverage Options: Inquire about any optional coverage or endorsements that may be available to enhance your insurance protection. This could include coverage for specific risks or additional coverage for valuable assets or specialized equipment.

5. Premiums and Payment Options: Understand the premium amounts and how they are calculated. Compare quotes from different insurance providers to ensure you are getting competitive rates. Inquire about payment options, such as annual, quarterly, or monthly installments, and assess the affordability of the premiums for your business.

6. Insurance Provider Reputation and Financial Stability: Research the insurance provider's reputation and financial stability. Check their ratings with independent rating agencies to ensure they have a strong financial standing and a history of reliable claims payment.

7. Professional Assistance: Seek guidance from insurance agents or brokers who specialize in small business insurance. They can help assess your business's unique risks, recommend appropriate coverage options, and navigate the insurance marketplace to find the best policies for your needs.

Remember to periodically review your insurance coverage as your business evolves. Changes in operations, expansions, or new risks may require adjustments to your insurance policies. Regularly assess your coverage needs and consult with insurance professionals to ensure your business is adequately protected.

Absolutely! By assessing your insurance needs, obtaining the appropriate coverage, and implementing risk management strategies, you can protect your business from unforeseen events, liabilities, and financial losses. Here are some key steps to consider:

1. Assess Your Risks: Identify the specific risks your business faces, such as property damage, liability claims, data breaches, or business interruptions. Consider the nature of your industry, location, and operations to understand the risks unique to your business.

2. Determine Required Coverage: Based on your risk assessment, determine the types of insurance coverage you need. Common types include general liability insurance, professional liability insurance, property insurance, cyber liability insurance, and workers' compensation insurance. Consult with insurance professionals to understand the specific coverage requirements for your industry and location.

3. Seek Reputable Insurance Providers: Research and select reputable insurance providers with experience in your industry. Consider their financial strength, customer reviews, and claims handling reputation. Work with an insurance agent or broker who can help you navigate the insurance marketplace and find the best coverage options for your business.

4. Review Policy Terms and Conditions: Carefully review the terms and conditions of your insurance policies. Understand the coverage limits, deductibles, exclusions, and any additional requirements or obligations. Ensure the policies align with your specific needs and provide adequate protection for your business.

5. Implement Risk Management Strategies: In addition to insurance, implement risk management strategies to minimize potential risks. This may include safety protocols, employee training, security measures, and disaster preparedness plans. The goal is to prevent or mitigate risks before they occur.

6. Regularly Assess and Update Coverage: As your business evolves, regularly assess your insurance needs. Changes in operations, expansions, or new ventures may require adjustments to your coverage. Review your policies annually or when significant changes occur to ensure your coverage remains appropriate and up to date.

7. Seek Professional Advice: Insurance can be complex, so consider seeking advice from insurance professionals or consultants who specialize in small business insurance. They can provide expert guidance, help you understand your coverage options, and ensure you have the right policies in place.

Chapter 12:

Exit Strategies and Succession Planning

Planning for the future of your business beyond your ownership is essential for long-term success. This chapter explores key considerations in developing exit strategies and succession plans, ensuring a smooth transition and maximizing the value of your business.

Understanding different exit strategies for business owners:

When considering exit strategies for your business, it's important to explore and understand the various options available. One option is selling the business, which involves finding a buyer who is willing to acquire your business and negotiating a sale price and terms. This can provide you with a financial return on your investment and allow you to move on to other ventures. However, selling a business can be a complex process that requires careful planning and preparation.

Another option is transferring ownership to family members or key employees. This allows you to keep the business within the family or reward loyal and talented employees by giving them the opportunity to take over the business. Succession planning and effective communication are crucial for a smooth transition and ensuring the long-term success of the business.

Merging with another company can be an attractive option as it allows you to combine resources, expertise, and market share. This can lead to increased growth opportunities and expanded market presence. However, merging with another company requires careful due diligence, negotiation, and integration planning to ensure a successful partnership.

If your business has the potential for significant growth and meets the requirements, pursuing an initial public offering (IPO) can provide access to capital markets and allow you to raise funds by selling shares to the public. However, going public is a complex and highly regulated process that requires significant financial and legal resources.

Other exit strategies include liquidation, where the business is closed and its assets are sold to pay off debts or distribute to owners, and management buyouts, where key employees or management purchase the business. These options may be suitable in certain circumstances, such as when the business is no longer viable or when key employees have the capability and desire to take ownership.

When evaluating exit strategies, it's important to consider your business goals, financial considerations, personal preferences, and the specific characteristics of your industry and market. Seeking advice from business advisors, legal professionals, and financial experts can help you assess the advantages, disadvantages, and feasibility of each option and make an informed decision that aligns with your objectives.

Planning for retirement and business continuity:

Retirement planning is a crucial aspect of an exit strategy for business owners. As you prepare to transition out of your business, it's important to consider how the business will continue to operate and thrive in your absence. Developing a succession plan is key to ensuring a smooth transition of leadership and maintaining business continuity.

Start by identifying potential successors within your organization who have the necessary skills, knowledge, and experience to take over the reins. This may involve grooming and developing key employees to assume leadership roles. Alternatively, you may need to consider external hires if there are no suitable internal candidates. Evaluate the strengths and weaknesses of potential successors and assess their fit with the company's long-term vision and values.

Communicate your succession plan to key stakeholders, including employees, clients, and business partners. Open and transparent communication is essential for instilling confidence in the future of the business and managing expectations. It can also help minimize disruptions and maintain employee morale during the transition.

Consider involving a trusted advisory team, which may include legal professionals, financial advisors, and business consultants, to guide you through the succession planning process. They can provide valuable insights, help you navigate legal and financial considerations, and ensure that the transition is executed in a legally compliant manner.

As part of your retirement planning, also take into account your personal financial needs. Assess your financial situation and consult with a financial advisor to develop a retirement plan that aligns with your goals and aspirations. Consider how the sale or transfer of the business will impact your financial security and explore strategies for managing your personal wealth and investments beyond the business.

Ultimately, incorporating retirement planning and developing a succession plan are essential components of a comprehensive exit strategy. By carefully considering the future of your business and taking proactive steps to ensure a smooth transition, you can set yourself up for a successful and fulfilling retirement while safeguarding the legacy of your business.

Selling the business and maximizing value:

When selling your business as part of your exit strategy, it is crucial to prepare the business to maximize its value and appeal to potential buyers. Start by enhancing profitability and streamlining operations to showcase the business's financial health and growth potential. Identify areas for improvement and implement strategies to increase efficiency and reduce costs.

Strengthening customer relationships is another important aspect of preparing your business for sale. Focus on providing exceptional customer service, building long-term customer loyalty, and diversifying your customer base. A strong and loyal customer base can be an attractive asset to potential buyers.

Conducting a thorough valuation of your business is essential to determine its fair market value. Engage professionals, such as business brokers or investment bankers, who have experience in business valuations and sales. They can help assess the financials, assets, intellectual property, and market position of your business to determine an appropriate asking price.

Prepare a comprehensive information memorandum or prospectus that provides potential buyers with a detailed overview of your business. This document should highlight its strengths, growth prospects, financial performance, and unique selling points. It is important to present accurate and transparent information to build trust with potential buyers.

Confidentiality is critical during the sales process to protect the sensitive information of your business. Implement strict confidentiality agreements and carefully vet potential buyers to ensure they are serious and qualified. Work closely with your advisory team to manage the flow of information and conduct due diligence on potential buyers.

Negotiating the sale of your business requires careful consideration of the terms and conditions. Seek professional advice to navigate the negotiation process and ensure that the sale agreement aligns with your financial and non-financial objectives. This may include the purchase price, payment terms, transition period, and any ongoing involvement you may have in the business post-sale.

Throughout the sales process, maintain open and transparent communication with potential buyers and your advisory team. Respond promptly to inquiries, provide requested information, and address concerns professionally. Building rapport and trust with potential buyers can facilitate a successful sale transaction.

Remember to consult with legal and financial professionals throughout the sales process to ensure compliance with legal requirements, minimize tax implications, and protect your interests. Their expertise and guidance can be invaluable in navigating the complexities of selling a business.

By preparing your business for sale, conducting a thorough valuation, engaging professionals, and negotiating the sale agreement, you can maximize the value of your business and facilitate a successful exit from the business.

Transferring ownership to family or key employees:

When transferring ownership of your business to family members or key employees, thorough planning and consideration of various factors are crucial for a smooth and successful transition. Start by identifying potential successors within your family or among your key employees who have the necessary skills, knowledge, and commitment to take over the business.

Develop a comprehensive plan for training and mentoring the chosen successors. Provide them with opportunities to gain hands-on experience and gradually assume more responsibilities within the business. This can involve cross-training in different departments, mentoring by current owners or key executives, and exposure to decision-making processes.

Consider the legal and financial implications of the ownership transfer. Consult with legal and financial professionals to determine the most appropriate structure for the transfer, such as a sale, gift, or combination of both. Address any potential tax consequences and explore strategies to minimize tax liabilities for both parties involved.

Family dynamics can play a significant role in the transfer of ownership. Open and transparent communication among family members is essential to ensure mutual understanding and agreement on the terms of the transfer. Consider involving a neutral third party, such as a family business advisor or mediator, to facilitate discussions and help navigate potential conflicts.

Create a succession plan that outlines the timeline, roles and responsibilities, and decision-making processes for the transfer of ownership. It should also address how the departing owner will be compensated and how the ongoing management and leadership of the business will be structured.

Maintain ongoing communication with all stakeholders involved in the ownership transfer process. Regularly update them on the progress and address any concerns or questions they may have. By keeping everyone informed and engaged, you can mitigate potential issues and foster a smooth transition.

Seek professional advice throughout the transfer process. Attorneys specializing in business and estate planning can assist with legal documentation, succession planning, and tax considerations. Financial advisors can provide guidance on valuing the business, structuring the transfer, and managing financial aspects of the transition.

Review and update your personal estate planning documents to align with the transfer of ownership. Ensure that your will, trusts, and other estate planning instruments reflect your intentions regarding the business transfer and address the needs of your family members or other beneficiaries.

Ultimately, the successful transfer of ownership to family members or key employees requires careful planning, clear communication, and professional guidance. By addressing legal, financial, and family dynamics considerations, you can ensure a smooth transition of ownership and set the stage for the continued success of your business.

Merging or acquiring another business:

When considering a merger or acquisition as part of your exit strategy, it is essential to conduct thorough due diligence to assess the potential benefits, risks, and compatibility of the target business. Due diligence should encompass financial, legal, operational, and cultural aspects to gain a comprehensive understanding of the target business and identify any potential issues or challenges.

Financial due diligence involves reviewing the target company's financial statements, tax records, and contracts to assess its financial health, profitability, and potential risks. Engage with financial experts, such as accountants or financial analysts, to conduct a detailed analysis of the target company's financials and evaluate the financial impact of the merger or acquisition.

Legal due diligence focuses on assessing the legal compliance and potential liabilities of the target company. Review contracts, licenses, permits, intellectual property rights, litigation history, and any regulatory or compliance issues. Engage with legal professionals experienced in mergers and acquisitions to identify and mitigate legal risks.

Operational due diligence involves evaluating the target company's operational capabilities, processes, and systems. Assess the compatibility of business operations, supply chains, distribution networks, and technology infrastructure. Identify any potential synergies or challenges that may arise from integrating the two businesses.

Cultural due diligence is essential to assess the compatibility of organizational cultures, values, and leadership styles. Understand the target company's corporate culture, employee morale, and management philosophy. Evaluate whether there is alignment and potential challenges in integrating the two cultures.

Develop a comprehensive integration plan to ensure a smooth transition and maximize the value of the merger or acquisition. This plan should include clear objectives, timelines, and responsibilities for integrating systems, processes, employees, and customers. Communication is key during this process to address any concerns and maintain the trust of employees, customers, and other stakeholders.

Engage with professionals experienced in mergers and acquisitions, such as investment bankers or business brokers, to guide you through the process. They can provide valuable insights, negotiate favorable terms, and facilitate a successful transaction.

Consider the financial and tax implications of the merger or acquisition. Consult with financial advisors and tax professionals to understand the impact on your financial statements, tax liabilities, and potential synergies that may lead to cost savings or increased revenues.

Keep in mind that mergers and acquisitions can be complex and time-consuming processes. It is important to be patient, flexible, and open to adjustments along the way. A well-executed merger or acquisition can provide growth opportunities, enhance competitiveness, and create value for your business, but careful planning, due diligence, and professional guidance are essential for a successful outcome.

Succession planning and leadership development:

Succession planning is a crucial aspect of preparing for the future of your business. It involves identifying and developing individuals within your organization who have the potential to take on key leadership roles. By implementing effective succession planning strategies, you can ensure a smooth transition of leadership and maintain business continuity.

Start by identifying high-potential employees who demonstrate the necessary skills, competencies, and qualities for future leadership positions. This can be done through talent assessment processes, performance evaluations, and feedback from managers and colleagues. Look for individuals who not only excel in their current roles but also display leadership potential, strong decision-making abilities, and a commitment to the organization's values and vision.

Once potential successors are identified, invest in their development through leadership training programs, mentorship opportunities, and targeted learning experiences. Provide them with exposure to different areas of the business, cross-functional projects, and opportunities to develop their skills and knowledge. Encourage them to take on stretch assignments and provide constructive feedback to support their growth.

Create a culture of growth and continuous learning within your organization. Encourage employees at all levels to pursue professional development and provide resources for ongoing learning and skill-building. Offer mentorship programs that pair emerging leaders with experienced executives who can provide guidance, support, and valuable insights.

Communicate openly and transparently with potential successors about their career paths and the organization's succession planning initiatives.

Provide regular feedback, set clear expectations, and help them understand the skills and experiences needed to advance in their careers. This will not only motivate and engage potential successors but also foster a sense of loyalty and commitment to the organization.

As part of succession planning, it is important to involve key stakeholders, such as board members, senior executives, and current business owners. Engage in conversations about long-term business goals, leadership needs, and potential transition timelines. This collaborative approach ensures alignment and smooth decision-making when it comes to selecting and preparing future leaders.

Consider external hires as part of your succession planning strategy. Assess the skills and expertise needed for future leadership roles and determine whether they can be fulfilled by internal candidates or if external recruitment is necessary. A balanced approach that combines internal talent development and external hiring can bring fresh perspectives and experiences to the organization.

Succession planning is an ongoing process that requires regular review and adjustment. As business needs evolve, continuously reassess the potential successors and adapt development plans accordingly. Regularly review and update your succession plan to ensure it remains aligned with the strategic direction of the business.

Engage with HR professionals, talent development experts, or executive coaches to assist with succession planning initiatives. They can provide expertise, guidance, and best practices to support the development of future leaders and ensure a successful transition of leadership within your organization.

By investing in succession planning and developing a pipeline of talented individuals, you can secure the long-term success and sustainability of your business. Effective succession planning allows for a seamless transition of leadership, ensures the continuity of operations, and positions your organization for continued growth and success.

Tax considerations in exit planning:

When developing your exit strategy, it is essential to consider the tax implications associated with your chosen path. Different exit strategies can have varying tax consequences, and understanding these implications can help you optimize your tax planning, minimize tax liabilities, and potentially take advantage of tax benefits.

To ensure you navigate the complex tax landscape effectively, it is advisable to consult with tax professionals, such as accountants or tax attorneys, who specialize in business taxation. They can provide valuable insights and guidance tailored to your specific situation, helping you make informed decisions.

Tax professionals can assess your business's financial position and goals, analyze the tax implications of different exit strategies, and provide advice on structuring the transaction in a tax-efficient manner. They can help you understand the tax consequences of selling or transferring ownership, merging with another company, or pursuing an IPO.

Additionally, tax professionals can help you identify any available tax benefits or incentives that may apply to your particular situation. They stay up to date with changes in tax laws and regulations, ensuring that your exit strategy remains compliant with the latest requirements.

By working closely with tax professionals, you can develop a comprehensive tax strategy that aligns with your business goals and helps you achieve the most favorable tax outcome. They can help you understand the potential tax liabilities associated with different exit scenarios, identify strategies to minimize taxes, and guide you through the tax compliance process.

It is crucial to engage with tax professionals early in the exit planning process. This allows for adequate time to assess your options, structure the transaction appropriately, and make any necessary adjustments to optimize your tax position. Waiting until the last minute may limit your ability to implement effective tax planning strategies.

Tax professionals can also assist with post-exit tax planning, helping you navigate any tax implications that may arise after the transaction is complete. This includes providing guidance on tax reporting requirements, managing any potential audits or inquiries from tax authorities, and ensuring ongoing tax compliance.

In summary, understanding the tax implications of your chosen exit strategy is vital to maximize the financial outcome and minimize tax liabilities. Engaging with tax professionals who specialize in business taxation can provide the expertise and guidance necessary to develop a sound tax strategy. By working closely with these professionals, you can optimize your tax planning, ensure compliance with tax laws and regulations, and achieve a successful and tax-efficient exit from your business..

Legal considerations during the transition process:

When executing your exit strategy, it is crucial to engage legal professionals experienced in business transactions to navigate the complex legal landscape. These professionals can provide valuable guidance and expertise to ensure compliance with contractual obligations, protect your interests, and address any legal issues that may arise during the transition.

One important aspect of your exit strategy is to review and understand any contractual obligations you have entered into. Legal professionals can help you assess your existing contracts, such as leases, vendor agreements, and customer contracts, to ensure compliance with termination or assignment provisions. They can also guide you in negotiating and drafting necessary agreements to facilitate a smooth transition of ownership or control.

Non-compete agreements are another critical consideration during an exit strategy. If you are selling your business or transferring ownership, it is essential to review and enforce non-compete agreements with key employees or shareholders to protect the value of your business. Legal professionals can assist in drafting, reviewing, or enforcing these agreements to safeguard your business's goodwill and prevent unfair competition.

Intellectual property protection is another area where legal professionals play a crucial role in the exit process. They can help identify and protect your intellectual property rights, including trademarks, copyrights, patents, and trade secrets. This includes conducting intellectual property audits, assessing licensing agreements, and ensuring that proper assignments or licenses are in place during the transition.

Legal professionals can also assist in addressing any potential legal issues that may arise during the exit process. This may involve conducting due diligence on potential legal risks, resolving contractual disputes, addressing employee-related matters, or handling regulatory compliance issues. Their expertise and advice can help mitigate legal risks and ensure a smooth and legally compliant exit.

In addition to addressing specific legal matters, legal professionals can provide strategic guidance throughout the entire exit process. They can help you evaluate different exit options, assess the legal implications of each choice, and provide guidance on structuring the transaction to maximize your desired outcomes.

By engaging legal professionals experienced in business transactions, you can navigate the legal complexities of your exit strategy with confidence. Their expertise can help you ensure compliance with contractual obligations, protect your intellectual property, address potential legal issues, and facilitate a successful transition. Their guidance is invaluable in safeguarding your interests and ensuring a legally sound exit from your business.

By developing a well-thought-out exit strategy and succession plan, you can ensure a smooth transition, maximize the value of your business, and preserve its legacy. Engage with professionals, such as business consultants, attorneys, and financial advisors, to assist in developing and executing your exit strategy. Regularly review and update your plan as circumstances change or new opportunities arise.

An effective exit strategy takes into account your long-term goals, financial considerations, and personal aspirations. It outlines a clear roadmap for transitioning out of your business, whether through a sale, transfer of ownership, merger, or other means. This strategy should align with your overall business objectives and provide a framework for achieving a successful exit.

Working with business consultants can provide valuable insights and expertise in crafting an exit strategy tailored to your specific circumstances. They can help you assess the market value of your business, identify potential buyers or successors, and develop a timeline for the transition process. Their guidance can ensure that you position your business for a successful exit, both financially and operationally.

Legal professionals, such as attorneys specializing in business transactions and succession planning, play a crucial role in executing your exit strategy. They can assist with legal due diligence, review and negotiate contracts and agreements, and ensure compliance with regulatory requirements. Attorneys can also provide guidance on tax implications and estate planning to optimize your financial outcomes and protect your personal interests.

Financial advisors can provide valuable insights into the financial aspects of your exit strategy. They can help you understand the potential tax implications, evaluate the financial impact of different exit options, and develop a comprehensive financial plan for your post-exit life. Their expertise in wealth management and investment strategies can help ensure that you make informed decisions and achieve your financial goals.

Regularly reviewing and updating your exit strategy is crucial as circumstances change. Market conditions, industry trends, personal circumstances, and the value of your business may fluctuate over time. By periodically reassessing your plan and engaging with professionals, you can make necessary adjustments and take advantage of new opportunities that may arise.

In conclusion, developing a well-crafted exit strategy and succession plan is essential for any business owner. Engaging with professionals, such as business consultants, attorneys, and financial advisors, can provide the expertise and guidance needed to navigate the complexities of the exit process. By regularly reviewing and updating your plan, you can ensure that it remains aligned with your goals and maximize the value of your business upon your exit.

Chapter 13:

Dispute Resolution and Legal Remedies

Disputes and conflicts are an inevitable part of running a business. Understanding various dispute resolution methods and legal remedies is crucial in effectively resolving conflicts and protecting your business's interests. This chapter explores key considerations in dispute resolution and pursuing legal remedies.

Understanding alternative dispute resolution methods:

Alternative dispute resolution (ADR) methods, such as mediation and arbitration, offer cost-effective alternatives to traditional litigation. Mediation involves a neutral third party assisting parties in reaching a mutually acceptable resolution. Arbitration involves a neutral arbitrator who makes a binding decision. Consider ADR as a way to resolve disputes without the expense and time associated with court proceedings.

Mediation is a collaborative process in which a trained mediator facilitates communication and negotiation between parties. The mediator helps parties identify their interests, explore potential solutions, and work towards a mutually agreeable resolution. Mediation allows for open dialogue and can often preserve relationships, making it particularly useful in resolving disputes involving ongoing business relationships.

Arbitration, on the other hand, is a more formal process in which parties present their cases to a neutral arbitrator who then renders a binding decision. Arbitration can be faster and less formal than traditional litigation, and the parties have more control over the process. It is commonly used when parties have agreed in advance to resolve disputes through arbitration, often as outlined in a contract or agreement.

Both mediation and arbitration can be advantageous in that they provide privacy, flexibility, and a more streamlined approach to resolving disputes. They can be particularly beneficial for complex business disputes, as they offer specialized expertise and allow parties to maintain more control over the outcome. Additionally, ADR methods are generally less costly and time-consuming than traditional litigation, making them attractive options for businesses seeking efficient resolution.

It is important to note that the success of ADR depends on the willingness of all parties to engage in good faith negotiation or abide by the decision of an arbitrator. While ADR can often result in mutually satisfactory outcomes, there may be instances where parties are unable to reach an agreement and resort to litigation.

To pursue ADR, parties can voluntarily agree to engage in mediation or arbitration, either before or after a dispute arises. In some cases, contracts or agreements may include provisions requiring or recommending ADR as the preferred method for dispute resolution.

In conclusion, alternative dispute resolution methods such as mediation and arbitration provide businesses with cost-effective and efficient alternatives to traditional litigation. These methods can help parties resolve disputes in a more collaborative and streamlined manner, while also preserving relationships and avoiding lengthy court proceedings. Consulting with an attorney experienced in ADR can provide guidance on the most appropriate method for your specific situation and help you navigate the process effectively.

Mediation and arbitration as cost-effective options:

Mediation and arbitration are alternative dispute resolution methods that offer efficient and cost-effective means of resolving disputes. These methods provide parties with the opportunity to maintain more control over the process and outcome, compared to traditional litigation.

In mediation, a neutral third party, known as a mediator, assists the parties in reaching a mutually acceptable resolution. The mediator facilitates communication, identifies common interests, and helps generate options for resolution. Mediation is a voluntary process that encourages open dialogue and promotes cooperation between the parties. It is a flexible and confidential method that allows for creative solutions tailored to the specific needs of the parties involved.

Arbitration, on the other hand, involves a neutral arbitrator or panel of arbitrators who render a binding decision after hearing arguments and evidence from both sides. The arbitrator's decision, known as an award, is typically final and enforceable. Arbitration can be less formal and more expedient than traditional litigation, and the rules of procedure can be tailored to the specific needs of the dispute.

When engaging in mediation or arbitration, it is important to select qualified professionals who have expertise in the subject matter of the dispute. Experienced mediators and arbitrators familiar with your industry or specific area of contention can bring valuable insight and help facilitate a fair and efficient resolution. They can guide the parties through the process, ensure procedural fairness, and promote productive communication.

Mediation and arbitration can be particularly beneficial for business disputes as they allow for more flexibility and confidentiality compared to court proceedings. They can help preserve ongoing business relationships and avoid the potential negative impact of a public trial. Additionally, these methods often result in faster resolutions and can be more cost-effective than traditional litigation.

It is essential to carefully consider the decision to engage in mediation or arbitration. Parties should assess the nature of the dispute, the desired outcome, and the willingness of all parties to participate in good faith. Consultation with legal counsel experienced in alternative dispute resolution can help assess the suitability of mediation or arbitration for your specific situation and guide you through the process effectively.

In conclusion, mediation and arbitration are valuable alternatives to litigation for resolving disputes. These methods offer parties greater control over the process, promote collaboration, and provide efficient and cost-effective resolutions. By engaging qualified professionals and approaching the process in good faith, parties can work towards a fair and satisfactory outcome that meets their interests and preserves relationships.

Navigating the small claims court system:

Small claims court can be an effective option for resolving smaller disputes involving limited monetary amounts. Each jurisdiction has its own rules and procedures for small claims court, so it is important to familiarize yourself with the specific requirements in your local area.

One advantage of small claims court is that it is designed to be more accessible and user-friendly compared to traditional court proceedings. The process is typically simpler, and parties are often allowed to represent themselves without the need for formal legal representation. This can reduce the costs and complexity associated with resolving disputes.

To pursue resolution through small claims court, it is important to thoroughly prepare your case. This involves gathering all relevant documentation and evidence to support your claims. This may include contracts, invoices, photographs, witness statements, or any other relevant materials that can help substantiate your position.

It is also essential to understand the jurisdictional limits of small claims court. Different jurisdictions have varying limits on the maximum monetary amount that can be claimed in small claims court. Make sure your dispute falls within these limits to be eligible for resolution in this forum.

When presenting your case in small claims court, it is important to clearly and concisely articulate your arguments and provide supporting evidence. Prepare a well-organized presentation that highlights the key facts and legal principles relevant to your case. Be prepared to respond to any questions or challenges from the judge.

While small claims court can be a cost-effective and efficient way to resolve smaller disputes, it is important to manage your expectations. The court's jurisdiction is typically limited to monetary damages, and there may be limitations on the types of claims that can be pursued. In some cases, the court's decision may be final and cannot be appealed.

Before proceeding to small claims court, it may be beneficial to explore alternative dispute resolution methods, such as negotiation or mediation, to try to resolve the dispute amicably. These methods can often lead to more mutually agreeable outcomes and preserve relationships.

In conclusion, small claims court can be a viable option for resolving smaller disputes involving limited monetary amounts. By understanding the rules and procedures specific to your local jurisdiction, thoroughly preparing your case, and presenting your arguments effectively, you can maximize your chances of success. However, it is important to consider alternative dispute resolution methods and seek legal advice when appropriate to determine the best course of action for your specific situation.

Pursuing legal action and civil litigation:

In certain situations, pursuing legal action through civil litigation may be necessary to protect your business's interests. If you believe that you have a valid claim or need to defend against a claim made against your business, it is advisable to consult with an attorney who specializes in business litigation.

An experienced business litigation attorney can assess the merits of your case, evaluate the evidence, and provide you with an analysis of the potential strengths and weaknesses. They will also help you understand the legal theories that may apply to your situation and the likelihood of success.

Before deciding to proceed with litigation, it is important to consider the potential costs, risks, and timeframes associated with this course of action. Litigation can be time-consuming, expensive, and emotionally draining. It is essential to weigh these factors against the potential benefits of pursuing a legal remedy.

Your attorney will guide you through the litigation process, which typically involves filing the necessary legal documents, engaging in the discovery process to gather evidence, negotiating with the opposing party, and, if necessary, presenting your case in court. They will represent your interests, advocate for you, and help navigate the complex legal procedures.

Throughout the litigation process, it is crucial to maintain open communication with your attorney and provide them with all relevant information and documents. This will enable them to build a strong case on your behalf and make informed decisions about the best strategies to pursue.

It is important to remember that litigation outcomes can be uncertain, as they depend on various factors, including the strength of the evidence, the arguments presented, and the judgment of the court or jury. While your attorney will work diligently to achieve a favorable outcome, there are no guarantees in litigation.

In some cases, alternative dispute resolution methods, such as negotiation, mediation, or arbitration, may be explored as alternatives to litigation. These methods can provide more efficient and cost-effective ways to resolve disputes while preserving relationships. Your attorney can help you assess whether these options are suitable for your specific situation.

In conclusion, civil litigation can be a complex and challenging process. By consulting with an experienced business litigation attorney, assessing the merits of your case, and considering the potential costs and risks, you can make an informed decision about pursuing legal action. Your attorney will provide guidance throughout the process and work diligently to protect your business's interests.

5. Enforcing contracts and collecting debts:

When facing contract breaches or difficulties collecting debts, explore legal remedies available to enforce contractual obligations. Send demand letters, engage in negotiations, or pursue legal actions, such as filing a lawsuit or seeking judgment. Understand the relevant laws, statutes of limitations, and legal processes for debt collection.

Intellectual property infringement claims:

If you believe that your business's intellectual property rights have been infringed upon, it is crucial to consult with an intellectual property attorney who specializes in this area of law. Intellectual property attorneys have the expertise and knowledge to assess the situation, understand the applicable laws, and guide you through the legal process.

When consulting with an intellectual property attorney, they will help you understand the legal remedies available to protect your intellectual property rights. These may include sending cease and desist letters to the infringing party, initiating negotiation or settlement discussions to resolve the matter amicably, or pursuing litigation if necessary.

Cease and desist letters are often the first step in addressing intellectual property infringement. These letters formally demand that the infringing party cease their infringing activities and provide an opportunity for them to respond and potentially resolve the matter without further legal action.

Negotiation can be a useful tool to reach a resolution that is satisfactory to both parties. Your attorney can assist in negotiating licensing agreements, settlement agreements, or other arrangements that address the infringement while protecting your intellectual property rights.

In some cases, litigation may be necessary to enforce your intellectual property rights. Your attorney will assess the strength of your case, gather evidence, and develop a legal strategy. They will represent your interests in court and seek legal remedies such as injunctions to stop the infringement, damages to compensate for losses, or other appropriate relief.

It is important to note that intellectual property litigation can be complex and time-consuming. The outcome of a legal dispute may depend on various factors, including the strength of your evidence, the applicable laws, and the judgment of the court. Your attorney will guide you through the process, explain the potential risks and costs, and help you make informed decisions.

Throughout the legal proceedings, it is vital to maintain open communication with your attorney, provide them with all relevant information and documentation, and follow their advice. They will work diligently to protect your intellectual property rights and achieve the best possible outcome for your business.

In conclusion, consulting with an intellectual property attorney is essential when dealing with intellectual property infringement. They will help you understand your legal options, guide you through the appropriate course of action, and work to protect your trademarks,

Defending against lawsuits and legal defenses:

If your business is facing a lawsuit, it is crucial to consult with an attorney who specializes in civil litigation. A skilled litigation attorney will have the knowledge and experience to assess the claims against your business, develop a strong defense strategy, and guide you through the legal process.

When consulting with a litigation attorney, they will carefully review the lawsuit and work with you to understand the allegations made against your business. They will gather evidence, examine relevant documents, and interview key witnesses to build a robust defense. Your attorney will also explore any available legal defenses that may apply to the specific claims raised in the lawsuit.

Settlement negotiations may be initiated at some point during the litigation process. Your attorney will assess the strength of your defense and the potential risks and costs of proceeding to trial. If a reasonable settlement can be reached that protects your business's interests, your attorney will guide you through the negotiation process and work to achieve a favorable outcome.

However, if a settlement cannot be reached or if it is not in your business's best interest, your attorney will be prepared to defend your interests in court. They will present your defense arguments, cross-examine witnesses, and present evidence to challenge the claims against your business. Throughout the litigation process, your attorney will keep you informed, provide legal advice, and advocate for your business's rights and interests.

It is important to note that civil litigation can be complex and time-consuming. The outcome of a lawsuit may depend on various factors, including the strength of your defense, the applicable laws, and the judgment of the court. Your attorney will work diligently to protect your business's interests and achieve the best possible outcome.

Throughout the litigation process, it is crucial to maintain open and ongoing communication with your attorney. Provide them with all relevant information and documentation, follow their advice, and be proactive in supporting your defense. By working closely with your attorney, you can navigate the legal process effectively and protect your business's reputation and financial well-being.

In conclusion, consulting with an experienced civil litigation attorney is essential if your business is sued. They will guide you through the defense process, develop a strong defense strategy, and advocate for your business's rights. Whether through negotiation or trial, your attorney will work to protect your interests and achieve a favorable resolution to the lawsuit.

Seeking legal advice and working with attorneys:

When encountering disputes or legal challenges, seeking the advice and representation of an experienced attorney is crucial. Attorneys possess the knowledge and expertise to guide you through the complexities of the legal system and provide you with tailored advice based on the specific circumstances of your case.

To find the right attorney, consider their experience and expertise in the relevant area of law. Look for attorneys who have a track record of success in handling similar cases or disputes. You may also seek recommendations from trusted sources, such as other business owners or professional networks.

During your initial consultation with an attorney, be prepared to discuss the details of your case openly and honestly. Provide them with all relevant documents, information, and any evidence you have. This will enable the attorney to evaluate the strength of your case and provide you with an informed assessment of your legal position and potential options.

Maintaining open and transparent communication with your attorney is essential. Be proactive in sharing any new developments, concerns, or questions you may have. A collaborative relationship with your attorney will ensure that you receive the best possible legal representation and that your attorney is fully equipped to advocate for your interests.

Follow the advice and guidance provided by your attorney. They will help you navigate the legal processes, prepare necessary documents, and represent your interests in negotiations or court proceedings. It is important to trust in their expertise and rely on their counsel throughout the legal process.

Remember that legal matters can take time and require patience. Your attorney will keep you informed about the progress of your case and explain any legal concepts or procedures that may be unfamiliar to you. By working closely with your attorney and maintaining open lines of communication, you can approach your legal challenges with confidence and maximize your chances of a favorable outcome.

In conclusion, consulting with an experienced attorney is essential when facing disputes or legal challenges. Their expertise and guidance will help you navigate the complexities of the legal system and advocate for your interests effectively. By establishing a collaborative relationship with your attorney and maintaining open communication, you can address your legal issues with confidence and achieve the best possible outcome.

By understanding alternative dispute resolution methods, pursuing legal remedies strategically, and working with experienced attorneys, you can navigate disputes effectively and protect your business's interests. Engaging legal professionals provides valuable guidance and support throughout the dispute resolution and litigation processes.

Alternative dispute resolution (ADR) methods such as mediation and arbitration offer efficient and cost-effective alternatives to traditional litigation. Mediation involves a neutral third party assisting parties in reaching a mutually acceptable resolution, while arbitration involves a neutral arbitrator making a binding decision. These methods allow parties to maintain more control over the process and outcome, and they often result in faster resolutions.

When pursuing legal action becomes necessary, consulting with an attorney experienced in the relevant area of law is essential. They can assess the merits of your case, develop a litigation strategy, and provide guidance on the legal procedures involved. An attorney will advocate for your interests, protect your rights, and work towards achieving a favorable resolution or outcome.

Working closely with your attorney, you can gather and present evidence, prepare legal arguments, and navigate the complexities of the legal system. They will guide you through the necessary steps, such as filing documents, responding to legal motions, and representing your interests in court proceedings.

Settlement negotiations may also be part of the dispute resolution process. Your attorney can assist in exploring settlement options, representing your interests, and helping you evaluate the potential benefits and risks involved. They will provide you with advice based on their legal expertise and experience, allowing you to make informed decisions.

In intellectual property disputes, such as trademark or copyright infringement, consulting with an intellectual property attorney is crucial. They can assess the situation, advise you on available legal remedies, and take appropriate action to protect your intellectual property rights. This may include sending cease and desist letters, engaging in negotiations, or pursuing litigation when necessary.

Throughout the dispute resolution process, maintaining open and transparent communication with your attorney is vital. Be proactive in sharing information, discussing your concerns, and asking questions. This will enable your attorney to provide you with the best possible advice and representation.

In conclusion, by understanding alternative dispute resolution methods, pursuing legal remedies strategically, and working with experienced attorneys, you can effectively navigate disputes and protect your business's interests. Engage legal professionals early in the process to receive guidance tailored to your specific situation and achieve the best possible resolution or outcome.

Chapter 14:

Ethical Considerations for Small Businesses

Ethical behavior and corporate social responsibility are essential for the long-term success and reputation of small businesses. This chapter explores key considerations in promoting ethical practices and cultivating an ethical culture within your organization.

Promoting ethical behavior and corporate social responsibility:

Embracing ethical behavior is crucial for building a reputable and socially responsible business. Start by developing a comprehensive code of ethics that outlines the expected standards of conduct for employees and stakeholders. This code should reflect your business values, promote integrity, honesty, and respect, and provide guidance on ethical decision-making.

Integrating corporate social responsibility (CSR) practices into your business operations is another way to demonstrate ethical behavior. Consider implementing sustainable practices that minimize environmental impact, such as reducing waste, conserving energy, or using eco-friendly materials. Engage in community involvement initiatives, such as volunteering, charitable donations, or partnerships with local organizations, to contribute positively to society.

Establishing a strong ethical culture within your business begins with leadership. Lead by example and demonstrate ethical behavior in your interactions with employees, customers, and business partners. Foster open communication channels where employees feel comfortable reporting ethical concerns or seeking guidance.

Ensure that employees receive training on ethical practices and understand the importance of upholding ethical standards. Provide ongoing education and reinforcement of ethical behavior through workshops, seminars, and regular communication. Encourage employees to ask questions and seek clarification when faced with ethical dilemmas.

Regularly assess your business practices and policies to ensure they align with ethical principles and legal requirements. Conduct internal audits or engage third-party assessments to evaluate compliance with ethical guidelines. Take prompt action to address any identified gaps or areas of concern.

Maintain transparency and accountability in your business operations. Communicate your ethical standards to customers, suppliers, and other stakeholders to build trust and foster long-term relationships. Be responsive to customer concerns or complaints and address them in a fair and timely manner.

Lastly, regularly review and update your code of ethics and CSR initiatives to reflect changing societal expectations and emerging ethical issues. Stay informed about industry-specific ethical guidelines and best practices to ensure your business remains current and adaptive.

In summary, embracing ethical behavior as a core value of your business is essential for long-term success and sustainability. Develop a code of ethics, integrate CSR practices, lead by example, provide training, assess compliance, and maintain transparency and accountability. By doing so, you can build a reputable business that not only drives profitability but also makes a positive impact on society.

Maintaining transparency and honest business practices:

Fostering a culture of transparency within your organization is essential for building trust and maintaining strong relationships with stakeholders. Begin by promoting open and honest communication at all levels of the company. Encourage employees to share their thoughts, ideas, and concerns, and provide them with a safe and supportive environment to do so.

Transparency should extend to your interactions with customers. Ensure that product descriptions and specifications are accurate and truthful, avoiding any misleading or deceptive information. Be transparent about pricing, including any additional fees or charges, to avoid surprises or misunderstandings. Honesty in marketing communications is also crucial, avoiding exaggerated claims or false representations.

Transparency should also be practiced in your relationships with suppliers and business partners. Clearly communicate your expectations, terms, and conditions, and ensure that agreements are documented in writing. Promptly address any issues or concerns that may arise, maintaining open lines of communication and working towards mutually beneficial resolutions.

Internally, provide employees with access to relevant information about the business, such as financial performance, goals, and strategic initiatives. This transparency helps employees understand the broader context of their work and fosters a sense of ownership and accountability.

In addition to communication, establish processes that promote transparency. For instance, implement clear policies and procedures that outline how decisions are made, how conflicts of interest are addressed, and how information is shared internally and externally. Regularly review and update these policies to ensure they remain relevant and aligned with your values and objectives.

Lead by example as a business leader by demonstrating transparency in your own actions and decisions. Share insights into your decision-making process and be open to feedback and constructive criticism. This approach helps to build credibility and trust with your employees, customers, and partners.

Transparency also involves being accountable for mistakes or errors. When a problem occurs, take responsibility, communicate openly about the issue, and outline the steps being taken to address it and prevent future occurrences. This proactive approach demonstrates your commitment to transparency and your willingness to learn from mistakes.

Regularly solicit feedback from stakeholders, such as through surveys, focus groups, or one-on-one conversations. Actively listen to their concerns, suggestions, and feedback and take appropriate action based on their input. This engagement demonstrates your commitment to transparency and your willingness to improve and adapt based on stakeholder perspectives.

By fostering a culture of transparency, you can create an environment where trust, collaboration, and integrity thrive. This not only benefits your organization internally but also enhances your reputation and relationships with customers, suppliers, and other stakeholders externally.

Avoiding conflicts of interest and bribery:

Maintaining integrity and avoiding conflicts of interest are vital for ethical business conduct. To achieve this, establish clear policies and procedures that address conflicts of interest within your organization. These policies should outline the types of situations that may create conflicts and provide guidelines on how to handle them.

Ensure that employees understand their responsibilities and obligations to act in the best interests of the business and avoid situations where personal interests may influence their decisions. Clearly communicate the importance of transparency, honesty, and ethical behavior in all aspects of the business.

Prohibit bribery and unethical practices in your policies, making it clear that such behavior will not be tolerated. Emphasize the importance of compliance with laws and regulations related to bribery, corruption, and other unethical activities. Implement internal controls and monitoring systems to detect and prevent any potential violations.

Promote a culture of ethical conduct by providing training and education to employees on ethical principles, conflict of interest, and proper business conduct. This training should emphasize the importance of integrity, ethical decision-making, and the consequences of non-compliance.

Establish a mechanism for employees to report potential conflicts of interest or unethical behavior, such as a confidential hotline or an anonymous reporting system. Encourage employees to report any concerns they may have and ensure that their reports are taken seriously and handled promptly and confidentially.

Regularly review and update your policies and procedures to address emerging ethical challenges and changes in laws and regulations. Seek input from employees, stakeholders, and legal professionals to ensure that your policies remain effective and aligned with best practices.

Lead by example as a business leader by demonstrating ethical behavior in your own actions and decisions. Uphold high standards of integrity and professionalism, and make it clear that ethical conduct is expected at all levels of the organization.

Conduct periodic audits or assessments to evaluate compliance with ethical standards and identify any areas of improvement. Use the findings to implement corrective actions and reinforce ethical behavior within the organization.

Lastly, collaborate with professional organizations, industry associations, and regulatory bodies to stay informed about best practices and evolving ethical standards in your industry. Engage in dialogue with peers to share experiences and learn from each other's approaches to ethical conduct.

By establishing clear policies, promoting ethical behavior, and addressing conflicts of interest, you can create a work environment that upholds integrity, protects against unethical practices, and ensures the best interests of the business are prioritized.

Ethical considerations in advertising and marketing:

Maintaining ethical standards in advertising and marketing is essential for building trust with consumers and promoting fair competition. To adhere to these standards:

Avoid deceptive or misleading practices in your advertising and marketing materials. Ensure that all claims made about your products or services are truthful, accurate, and substantiated. Provide clear and transparent information about the features, benefits, and limitations of your offerings.

Do not engage in unfair competition by disparaging competitors or engaging in dishonest tactics to gain an unfair advantage. Compete based on the merits of your products or services and strive to provide the best value to your customers.

Respect intellectual property rights by obtaining proper permissions or licenses when using copyrighted materials, trademarks, or other protected works. Avoid infringing on the intellectual property of others and clearly attribute any content or ideas that are not your own.

Maintain transparency in endorsements and sponsorships. Disclose any material connections or financial arrangements between your business and individuals or entities endorsing your products or services. Comply with the guidelines set forth by the Federal Trade Commission (FTC) regarding endorsements and testimonials.

Comply with applicable laws and regulations, including those established by the FTC. Familiarize yourself with guidelines related to advertising, endorsements, native advertising, and other relevant areas. Stay informed about changes or updates to these regulations and adjust your practices accordingly.

Ensure that your marketing materials are appropriate and respectful. Avoid using offensive or discriminatory language, imagery, or stereotypes. Respect consumer privacy and comply with data protection laws when collecting, storing, or using personal information.

Engage in responsible and ethical online marketing practices. Avoid spamming, phishing, or engaging in any form of online harassment. Be transparent about how you collect and use customer data and obtain proper consent when necessary.

Train your marketing team and employees on ethical marketing practices, providing them with clear guidelines and expectations. Foster a culture of ethics within your organization by encouraging open discussions, promoting ethical decision-making, and addressing any concerns or violations promptly.

Regularly review and assess your marketing materials, campaigns, and strategies to ensure they align with ethical standards. Seek feedback from customers, stakeholders, and legal professionals to gain different perspectives and make necessary improvements.

By adhering to ethical standards in advertising and marketing, you can build a positive reputation, establish trust with consumers, and contribute to a fair and responsible business environment.

Protecting customer privacy and data security:

Safeguarding customer privacy and protecting their personal data is of utmost importance in today's digital age. To ensure the privacy and security of customer information:

Implement robust data protection measures, including encryption, firewalls, and secure servers, to safeguard customer data from unauthorized access, hacking, or data breaches. Regularly update and patch your systems to address any vulnerabilities.

Adopt privacy by design principles, considering privacy and data protection from the early stages of product or service development. Implement privacy-enhancing technologies and practices that minimize the collection, storage, and processing of personal data to the extent necessary.

Comply with privacy regulations, such as the General Data Protection Regulation (GDPR) in the European Union or the California Consumer Privacy Act (CCPA) in the United States, if applicable to your business. Understand the requirements and obligations under these regulations and ensure your practices align with them.

Obtain appropriate consent from customers for the collection, use, and processing of their personal data. Clearly communicate the purposes for which data is collected and provide individuals with the option to opt out or withdraw their consent.

Be transparent about your data practices by providing a privacy policy that clearly explains how customer data is collected, used, stored, and shared. Include information on the types of data collected, the purposes for which it is used, and any third parties with whom it is shared.

Adhere to data retention policies and only retain customer data for as long as necessary. Regularly review and delete outdated or unnecessary customer data to minimize risks and ensure compliance with privacy regulations.

Educate your employees on data protection best practices and the importance of customer privacy. Implement internal policies and procedures to guide employees in handling and protecting customer data. Conduct regular training sessions to keep employees updated on privacy regulations and security measures.

Regularly monitor and audit your data protection practices to identify and address any vulnerabilities or non-compliance issues. Conduct risk assessments to identify potential threats and take appropriate measures to mitigate those risks.

In the event of a data breach or security incident, have a response plan in place. Act swiftly to contain the breach, notify affected individuals as required by law, and cooperate with relevant authorities. Take steps to rectify the situation and strengthen your security measures to prevent future incidents.

By prioritizing customer privacy and implementing strong data protection measures, you can build trust with your customers, comply with privacy regulations, and mitigate the risks associated with data breaches or unauthorized access.

Implementing fair employment practices:

Promoting fair and inclusive employment practices is crucial for creating a positive work environment and ensuring the well-being of your employees. Here are some key steps to follow:

Adhere to laws and regulations that promote equal opportunity and prohibit discrimination in the workplace, such as the Civil Rights Act of 1964, the Americans with Disabilities Act (ADA), and the Age

Discrimination in Employment Act (ADEA). Understand and comply with the requirements and protections outlined in these laws.

Develop and implement clear policies and procedures that promote fair treatment and equal opportunity for all employees. These policies should address issues such as hiring, promotion, compensation, benefits, and disciplinary actions. Regularly review and update these policies to reflect evolving legal requirements and best practices.

Ensure that your recruitment and selection processes are fair and unbiased. Avoid discriminatory practices, such as asking prohibited questions during interviews or making employment decisions based on protected characteristics such as race, gender, age, religion, or disability. Implement diversity and inclusion initiatives to attract and retain a diverse workforce.

Provide equal access to training, development opportunities, and advancement within the organization. Offer mentoring programs, career development plans, and opportunities for professional growth to all employees, regardless of their background or characteristics.

Maintain a workplace culture that values diversity, inclusion, and respect. Foster an environment where employees feel comfortable expressing their opinions, ideas, and concerns. Prohibit harassment, bullying, or any form of discriminatory behavior and promptly address any complaints or issues that arise.

Regularly assess and monitor your organization's practices and policies to identify and address any disparities or potential biases. Conduct periodic audits of your HR practices, compensation structures, and promotion processes to ensure fairness and equal treatment.

Provide training to managers and employees on diversity, inclusion, and unconscious bias to promote awareness and sensitivity. Encourage open dialogue and communication around these topics to foster understanding and respect among team members.

Encourage employee feedback and establish mechanisms for employees to report any concerns related to discrimination, harassment, or unfair treatment. Take all complaints seriously, conduct thorough investigations, and take appropriate action to address any substantiated issues.

By promoting fair and inclusive employment practices, you create a positive work environment that attracts and retains top talent, enhances employee morale and productivity, and positions your organization as a responsible and ethical employer.

Ethical considerations in supplier relationships:

Choosing ethical suppliers is an important aspect of maintaining ethical business practices. Here are some steps to consider when selecting suppliers:

Conduct thorough research and due diligence on potential suppliers. Evaluate their reputation, track record, and adherence to ethical standards. Look for certifications or memberships in organizations that promote fair labor practices, environmental sustainability, and social responsibility.

Consider the supplier's commitment to fair labor practices, such as providing safe working conditions, fair wages, and reasonable working hours for their employees. Assess their compliance with labor laws and regulations in their respective jurisdictions.

Evaluate the supplier's environmental practices and sustainability efforts. Look for suppliers that minimize their carbon footprint, promote resource conservation, and engage in responsible waste management. Consider their use of sustainable materials, energy-efficient processes, and commitment to reducing environmental impact.

Assess the supplier's commitment to social responsibility. Look for evidence of their involvement in community initiatives, charitable contributions, or partnerships with organizations dedicated to social causes. Consider their efforts to promote diversity, inclusion, and equality within their own organization.

Engage in open and transparent communication with potential suppliers. Discuss your expectations regarding ethical practices and ensure they align with your own values. Request information about their policies, codes of conduct, and certifications related to ethical standards.

Establish clear contractual agreements with suppliers that include provisions for ethical practices, labor standards, environmental sustainability, and social responsibility. Regularly monitor and assess their performance in these areas to ensure ongoing compliance.

Maintain open lines of communication with suppliers and encourage dialogue on ethical matters. Address any concerns or issues promptly and work collaboratively to find solutions that align with both parties' ethical standards.

Periodically review your supplier relationships and reassess their alignment with your ethical values. If ethical concerns arise, consider alternative suppliers that better meet your ethical criteria.

By choosing suppliers who share your ethical values, you contribute to the promotion of fair labor practices, environmental sustainability, and social responsibility throughout your supply chain. This not only supports your business's ethical reputation but also contributes to the overall advancement of responsible business practices in your industry.

Building a strong ethical culture within the organization:

Creating an ethical culture within your organization requires proactive efforts and strong leadership. Here are some steps you can take to promote ethical behavior:

Lead by example: As a business owner or leader, demonstrate ethical behavior in your actions and decision-making. Your commitment to ethical principles will set the tone for the entire organization.

Establish a code of ethics: Develop a code of ethics that outlines the values and standards expected from employees. Clearly communicate these expectations and ensure that employees understand the importance of adhering to ethical guidelines.

Implement ethics training programs: Provide regular ethics training to employees at all levels of the organization. These programs can educate employees on ethical principles, provide guidance on handling ethical dilemmas, and promote awareness of potential ethical issues.

Encourage open communication: Create an environment where employees feel comfortable reporting unethical behavior or raising ethical concerns. Establish channels, such as a confidential hotline or designated contact person, for employees to report any misconduct without fear of retaliation.

Reward ethical behavior: Recognize and reward employees who demonstrate ethical behavior and uphold the values of the organization. This encourages others to follow suit and reinforces the importance of ethics within the workplace.

Regularly assess and reinforce ethical practices: Conduct periodic assessments of ethical practices within the organization. This can include conducting ethics audits, reviewing policies and procedures, and addressing any identified gaps or areas for improvement. Continuously reinforce ethical standards through communication and ongoing training.

Address unethical behavior promptly: If unethical behavior is identified, take prompt and appropriate action to address the situation. This may involve conducting investigations, taking disciplinary measures, or implementing corrective actions to prevent recurrence.

Promote transparency and accountability: Foster a culture of transparency by providing employees with information about the organization's ethical practices, performance, and progress. Establish accountability mechanisms to ensure that ethical standards are upheld throughout the organization.

Regularly review and update ethical guidelines: As business practices and regulations evolve, regularly review and update your code of ethics and ethical guidelines to ensure they remain relevant and aligned with current standards and expectations.

By actively promoting ethical behavior, you create a positive work environment, build trust with stakeholders, and mitigate the risk of unethical conduct. Your commitment to ethics will not only benefit your organization but also contribute to the broader ethical standards within your industry and society as a whole.

By promoting ethical behavior, maintaining transparency, and implementing fair practices, you can cultivate a strong ethical culture within your small business. Incorporate ethical considerations into decision-making processes, policies, and practices at all levels of the organization. Regularly assess and update ethical guidelines to align with evolving societal expectations and legal requirements.

Chapter 15:

Resources and Support for Florida Small Businesses

Running a small business requires access to resources and support networks. In Florida, there are various avenues available to assist small business owners. This chapter explores key resources and support systems that can benefit Florida small businesses.

Utilizing government resources and programs:

As a small business owner, you can benefit from various government resources and programs that are designed to support and promote small businesses. Here are some avenues to explore:

U.S. Small Business Administration (SBA): The SBA offers a range of programs and services to assist small businesses, including access to capital through loans and grants, counseling and mentorship programs, government contracting opportunities, and disaster assistance. Visit the SBA's website (sba.gov) to learn more about the available resources and programs.

Florida Department of Economic Opportunity: The Florida Department of Economic Opportunity provides resources and programs to support small businesses in the state. They offer assistance in areas such as business development, financing, workforce training, and incentives for job creation. Visit their website or reach out to their local offices for more information on the specific programs available in Florida.

Local economic development agencies: Many local communities have economic development agencies or chambers of commerce that offer support and resources for small businesses. These organizations often provide networking opportunities, business development programs, and access to local funding or incentive programs. Contact your local economic development agency or chamber of commerce to inquire about the resources and programs available in your area.

Business incubators and accelerators: Business incubators and accelerators provide support to startups and early-stage businesses. They offer resources such as office space, mentoring, networking opportunities, and access to funding. Research and reach out to business incubators or accelerators in your area to explore potential opportunities for your business.

Small Business Development Centers (SBDCs): SBDCs are funded in part by the SBA and provide free or low-cost consulting and training services to small businesses. They offer guidance on various aspects of business development, including business planning, marketing, finance, and operations. Locate your nearest SBDC and inquire about their services and resources.

Trade associations and industry-specific organizations: Joining trade associations or industry-specific organizations can provide valuable networking opportunities, industry insights, and access to resources tailored to your specific sector. These organizations often offer educational programs, advocacy efforts, and platforms for business collaboration.

By taking advantage of government resources and programs, you can tap into valuable support, guidance, and funding opportunities that can contribute to the success and growth of your small business. Stay informed about the available resources and reach out to the relevant organizations to explore how they can assist you in achieving your business goals.

Engaging with local chambers of commerce and business associations:

Joining local chambers of commerce and business associations can be highly beneficial for small businesses. These organizations provide valuable networking opportunities, community involvement, and access to resources that can contribute to your business's growth and success. Here's why you should consider joining:

Networking opportunities: Chambers of commerce and business associations bring together business owners, professionals, and community leaders in your local area. By becoming a member, you gain access to networking events, meetings, and mixers where you can connect with other business professionals. These interactions can lead to valuable partnerships, collaborations, and potential customer referrals.

Community involvement: Chambers of commerce and business associations are often involved in community events, initiatives, and advocacy efforts. By joining, you can contribute to the betterment of your local community, showcase your business's commitment to the area, and build strong relationships with other community stakeholders.

Resources and support: Chambers of commerce and business associations provide resources and support to their members. This can include access to educational events, workshops, and seminars on various business topics, such as marketing, finance, and business development. Additionally, they may offer resources like business directories, member-to-member discounts, and promotional opportunities that can help you raise awareness and visibility for your business.

Advocacy and representation: These organizations often advocate on behalf of the business community, representing their interests and concerns to local government bodies and decision-makers. By being a member, you have a voice in shaping policies and regulations that impact your business. Chambers of commerce and business associations can also provide updates on relevant legislative changes and keep you informed about economic trends and opportunities.

Credibility and visibility: Membership in a local chamber of commerce or business association can enhance your business's credibility and visibility in the community. It signals that you are committed to the local economy and adhere to a certain standard of ethics and professionalism. Being associated with these organizations can instill trust in potential customers and business partners.

To join a local chamber of commerce or business association, reach out to them directly or visit their websites to learn about membership requirements and benefits. Consider attending their events or meetings as a guest to get a sense of the organization's culture and activities. Evaluate the offerings, costs, and alignment with your business goals before making a decision to join.

By joining these organizations, you can expand your network, gain access to valuable resources, and contribute to the growth and success of your business and local community.

Accessing small business development centers:

Small Business Development Centers (SBDCs) in Florida are valuable resources that can provide essential assistance to small business owners. Here's why you should consider utilizing their services:

Guidance and expertise: SBDCs offer guidance and expertise across various aspects of business development. Whether you need assistance with business planning, marketing strategies, financial analysis, or accessing capital, SBDCs have experienced advisors who can provide valuable insights and advice tailored to your specific business needs. They can help you develop and refine your business strategies to maximize your chances of success.

No-cost or low-cost assistance: One of the significant advantages of SBDCs is that they offer their services at little to no cost. As a small business owner, this can be incredibly beneficial, especially when you have limited financial resources. SBDC advisors are dedicated to supporting small businesses and are often funded through partnerships with government agencies, universities, and local organizations.

Access to resources: SBDCs provide access to a wide range of resources that can help you navigate the complexities of running a business. They can connect you with valuable tools, templates, and market research data that can assist in making informed business decisions. Additionally, they can help you identify and apply for grants, loans, or other funding opportunities available to small businesses.

Mentorship and networking: SBDCs often have a network of experienced business mentors who can provide guidance and support based on their own entrepreneurial journey. These mentors can offer practical insights, share their experiences, and provide valuable advice as you navigate the challenges of starting and growing your business. SBDCs may also facilitate networking events or workshops where you can connect with other entrepreneurs and business professionals.

Tailored assistance for growth and expansion: If your business is ready for growth or expansion, SBDCs can assist you with strategic planning and identifying opportunities for scaling your operations. They can help you analyze market trends, explore new markets, and develop strategies to reach your growth objectives. SBDCs can also provide guidance on accessing capital for expansion through loans, grants, or other financing options.

To access the services of SBDCs in Florida, visit their website or contact them directly. They will guide you through the process of engaging with an advisor who can assess your needs and provide the necessary support. It's important to take advantage of these resources to enhance your business's chances of success and to leverage the expertise and guidance available to you at no or low cost.

Remember, SBDCs are dedicated to helping small businesses thrive, and their services can be instrumental in your business's growth and development.

Tapping into mentorship and networking opportunities:

Mentorship can be a valuable resource for small business owners. Here are some ways you can seek mentorship opportunities and benefit from the wisdom and guidance of experienced entrepreneurs:

Local organizations and business associations: Many local organizations and business associations offer mentorship programs or can connect you with experienced entrepreneurs who are willing to share their knowledge and insights. These organizations often host networking events, seminars, and workshops where you can meet and connect with potential mentors. Reach out to these organizations in your area and inquire about mentorship opportunities they may have available.

Mentorship programs: Look for mentorship programs specifically designed for small business owners. These programs match you with mentors who have expertise in your industry or specific business challenges. Organizations such as SCORE (Service Corps of Retired Executives) and the Small Business Administration (SBA) offer mentorship programs that pair you with experienced business professionals who can provide guidance and support.

Industry-specific associations: Joining industry-specific associations can provide you with opportunities to connect with entrepreneurs who have experience and knowledge in your field. These associations often host conferences, seminars, and networking events where you can meet potential mentors. Engaging with industry peers and professionals can open doors to mentorship relationships and valuable insights.

Networking events: Attend local networking events and business conferences to expand your professional network and meet potential mentors. These events offer opportunities to engage with successful entrepreneurs who may be willing to share their experiences and offer guidance. Be proactive in building relationships and expressing your interest in mentorship.

Online platforms and communities: Explore online platforms and communities dedicated to entrepreneurship and small business. Platforms like LinkedIn, industry-specific forums, and business-focused social media groups provide spaces where you can connect with experienced professionals and seek mentorship opportunities. Engage in discussions, ask questions, and reach out to individuals who inspire you or possess the knowledge you seek.

When approaching potential mentors, be respectful of their time and expertise. Clearly communicate your goals, challenges, and expectations for the mentorship relationship. Establish a schedule for meetings or check-ins and come prepared with specific questions or topics you would like to discuss. Remember, mentorship is a two-way street, so be open to learning and actively apply the insights and advice you receive.

Building a mentorship relationship takes time and effort, so be patient and persistent. Remember to express gratitude for the guidance and support you receive from your mentor. Mentorship can be a valuable resource in your entrepreneurial journey, providing you with valuable perspectives, guidance, and encouragement to navigate challenges and achieve your business goals.

Seeking professional guidance from attorneys and consultants:

Engaging professionals who specialize in small business matters can be instrumental in ensuring legal compliance, navigating complex regulations, and developing effective business strategies. Here are some steps to help you find and engage the right professionals for your business:

Referrals and recommendations: Seek referrals from other small business owners, colleagues, or industry contacts who have had positive experiences with professionals in the specific areas you require assistance. Personal recommendations can provide valuable insights into the expertise, professionalism, and effectiveness of a professional.

Online research and reviews: Conduct online research to identify professionals who specialize in small business matters. Explore their websites, review their credentials, and look for client testimonials or reviews to gauge their reputation and track record. Online directories and platforms specific to your industry or location can also be helpful resources.

Consultations and interviews: Once you have identified potential professionals, schedule consultations or interviews to discuss your specific needs and assess their suitability for your business. Prepare a list of questions to ask, focusing on their experience working with small businesses, their understanding of your industry, and their approach to providing services.

Specialized expertise: Consider the specific expertise you require from the professional. For legal matters, seek attorneys who specialize in small business law, intellectual property, contracts, or other relevant areas. For consulting services, look for professionals with experience in areas such as business development, marketing, finance, or operations.

Compatibility and communication: Evaluate the compatibility and communication style of the professional. It is important to work with someone who understands your business goals, communicates effectively, and is responsive to your needs. Establish clear expectations regarding timelines, deliverables, and fees to ensure a mutually beneficial working relationship.

Cost and affordability: Discuss the fees and payment structure upfront to ensure that the professional's services align with your budget. Consider the value and expertise they bring to the table and weigh it against the cost to make an informed decision.

Engaging professionals who specialize in small business matters can provide valuable guidance and support, helping you navigate legal complexities, optimize business operations, and achieve your goals. By selecting the right professionals for your specific needs, you can benefit from their expertise and focus on driving your business forward.

Staying updated on legal and regulatory changes:

Staying informed about legal and regulatory changes is crucial for maintaining compliance and adapting to the evolving business landscape. Here are some strategies to help you stay up to date:

Government websites: Regularly visit relevant government websites, such as the U.S. Small Business Administration (SBA), the Internal Revenue Service (IRS), and the Federal Trade Commission (FTC). These websites often provide updates on new regulations, changes in tax laws, and other important information for small businesses.

Industry publications: Subscribe to industry-specific publications or newsletters that cover legal and regulatory topics relevant to your business. These publications often provide insights, analysis, and updates on changes in laws and regulations that may impact your industry.

Professional associations: Join industry-specific professional associations or trade organizations that offer resources, educational materials, and updates on legal and regulatory matters. Attend conferences, seminars, and webinars hosted by these associations to stay informed and network with other professionals in your field.

Legal professionals: Maintain a relationship with legal professionals who specialize in your industry or small business matters. Schedule periodic consultations or retain their services to receive updates on legal changes and guidance on compliance. Engage them to conduct regular audits of your business practices and contracts to ensure ongoing compliance.

Networking and peer groups: Engage in networking activities, both online and offline, to connect with other small business owners and professionals in your industry. Participate in peer groups or online forums where members share insights and updates on legal and regulatory changes.

Continuing education: Attend workshops, seminars, or webinars focused on legal and regulatory topics for small businesses. These educational programs provide valuable information and updates on changes in laws and regulations, as well as guidance on compliance and best practices.

Regular internal reviews: Establish a process within your business to regularly review and assess legal and regulatory compliance. Assign someone in your organization to monitor updates and changes, and disseminate relevant information to the appropriate teams or departments.

By proactively staying informed about legal and regulatory changes, you can ensure that your business remains compliant and prepared for any shifts in the legal landscape. Regularly consult with legal professionals and industry resources to understand how these changes may impact your operations and take appropriate action to adapt and comply.

Continuing education and professional development:

Continuing your professional development is essential for staying competitive and growing your business. Here are some ways to invest in your professional development:

Training programs and workshops: Look for training programs or workshops that offer practical skills and knowledge relevant to your industry or business needs. These programs can cover a wide range of topics, such as leadership development, marketing strategies, financial management, or digital skills. Participating in such programs can enhance your expertise and help you stay up to date with industry best practices.

Industry conferences and webinars: Attend industry conferences, trade shows, or webinars to stay updated on the latest trends, innovations, and challenges in your field. These events often feature expert speakers, panel discussions, and networking opportunities that can provide valuable insights and connections.

Online courses and certifications: Explore online platforms that offer courses and certifications in areas relevant to your business. This could include marketing, finance, project management, data analytics, or entrepreneurship. Online courses provide flexibility and allow you to learn at your own pace while acquiring new skills and knowledge.

Industry associations and organizations: Join professional associations or organizations specific to your industry. These groups often offer educational resources, webinars, and networking opportunities that can help you stay informed and connected with others in your field.

Mentorship programs: Seek out mentorship opportunities where experienced professionals in your industry can provide guidance and support. Mentors can share valuable insights, offer advice, and help you navigate challenges based on their own experiences.

Business incubators and accelerators: Consider joining a business incubator or accelerator program that provides support, resources, and mentoring to startups and small businesses. These programs often offer educational workshops, access to industry experts, and networking opportunities with other entrepreneurs.

Personal development books and podcasts: Explore books, podcasts, and other media that offer insights into business strategies, leadership development, and personal growth. These resources can provide inspiration and practical advice that can be applied to your business.

Remember, investing in your professional development is an ongoing process. Set aside dedicated time and resources to continuously learn, grow, and adapt to changes in your industry. By expanding your skills and knowledge, you can position yourself and your business for long-term success.

Online tools and resources for small business owners:

Harnessing the power of online tools and resources can greatly benefit your small business. Here are some ways you can take advantage of these resources:

Business templates: Online platforms provide a wide range of business templates that can save you time and effort. These templates include business plans, financial statements, marketing plans, employee contracts, and more. Utilizing these templates can help you create professional documents and streamline your business processes.

Financial calculators: Online financial calculators can assist you in making important financial decisions. These calculators can help you with cash flow projections, loan repayments, budgeting, and investment analysis. By using these tools, you can make informed financial decisions that align with your business goals.

Marketing resources: Online platforms offer marketing resources such as guides, tutorials, and templates to help you create effective marketing strategies. These resources cover various aspects of marketing, including social media, content marketing, email campaigns, and SEO. Leveraging these resources can help you reach your target audience and grow your customer base.

Educational materials: Online learning platforms provide access to a wide range of educational materials tailored to business owners. You can find courses, webinars, and e-books covering topics such as business strategy, sales and marketing, finance, and leadership. These resources allow you to enhance your knowledge and skills on your own schedule.

Online communities and forums: Engaging with online communities and forums specific to your industry or business niche can be valuable. These platforms provide opportunities to connect with like-minded entrepreneurs, share insights and experiences, and seek advice or recommendations. Participating in these communities can expand your network and provide a support system of fellow business owners.

Online marketplaces: Consider utilizing online marketplaces to reach a broader customer base or find suppliers for your business. Platforms such as Amazon, eBay, Etsy, or Shopify can provide a platform to sell your products online. Additionally, you can find suppliers or source materials through online marketplaces specific to your industry.

By leveraging online tools and resources, you can access valuable information, streamline your processes, and connect with a broader business community. Take advantage of these resources to enhance your business operations and stay competitive in the digital age.

Taking advantage of the resources and support available to small business owners in Florida can greatly contribute to the success and growth of your business. By tapping into government resources, such as those offered by the Small Business Administration (SBA) and the Florida Department of Economic Opportunity, you can access valuable programs, funding options, and business development resources.

Engaging with local chambers of commerce, business associations, and networking events allows you to connect with fellow entrepreneurs, gain insights, and establish valuable relationships. These organizations often offer educational events, workshops, and opportunities for collaboration and community involvement.

Small business development centers (SBDCs) provide valuable assistance and guidance to small business owners. Their services range from business planning and financial analysis to marketing strategies and accessing capital. Working with SBDCs can provide you with the support and expertise needed to navigate the challenges of running a small business.

Seeking mentorship opportunities allows you to learn from experienced entrepreneurs who can provide guidance and support based on their own business journeys. Mentorship programs, industry-specific organizations, and networking events can help you connect with mentors and peers who can offer valuable insights and advice.

Engaging professionals, such as attorneys and consultants, who specialize in small business matters can provide you with expert advice and guidance on legal, regulatory, and strategic matters. These professionals can help ensure compliance with laws and regulations, offer solutions to challenges, and provide valuable insights into growing and managing your business.

Staying informed about legal and regulatory changes is crucial to running a successful business. Regularly reviewing government websites, industry publications, and consulting with legal professionals keeps you up to date with any changes that may impact your operations. This allows you to adapt and make informed decisions to stay compliant and ahead of the curve.

Investing in your professional development through training programs, workshops, and online courses helps you enhance your skills and knowledge. By continuously learning and staying abreast of industry trends and best practices, you can position yourself and your business for long-term success.

By leveraging these resources, networking with fellow business owners, and investing in your own development, you can access the support and knowledge needed to overcome challenges, seize opportunities, and achieve your business goals.

Chapter 16:

Conclusion

Starting and operating a small business in Florida requires careful planning, knowledge of legal obligations, and a commitment to ethical practices. In this comprehensive guide, we have explored various aspects of running a small business, providing insights and expert advice to help you navigate the challenges and maximize your chances of success.

Throughout the book, we have covered a wide range of topics relevant to Florida small businesses. From legal considerations and compliance with regulations to financial management, marketing, and employee relations, each chapter has provided valuable information to guide you through the intricacies of starting and running a business.

We discussed the importance of registering your business, understanding tax obligations, and complying with licensing requirements. We explored the significance of intellectual property protection, marketing compliance, and online business practices. We also addressed key considerations such as employment and labor laws, contracts and legal agreements, and risk management.

Additionally, we highlighted the importance of ethical practices, corporate social responsibility, and building a strong ethical culture within your organization. We emphasized the significance of engaging with resources and support systems available to Florida small businesses, including government programs, business associations, small business development centers, and professional guidance.

As a small business owner, you have embarked on an exciting and challenging journey. By applying the knowledge and insights shared in this book, you are better equipped to navigate legal complexities, make informed decisions, and overcome obstacles that may arise along the way.

Remember, success in business is not achieved in isolation. Engaging with mentors, networking with other entrepreneurs, and seeking professional guidance can provide invaluable support and guidance throughout your journey. Stay updated on legal and regulatory changes, continue to learn and develop your skills, and adapt your strategies to the evolving business landscape.

Starting and operating a small business requires dedication, resilience, and a commitment to continuous improvement. With careful planning, a strong ethical foundation, and access to the resources and support systems available, you are well on your way to achieving your entrepreneurial goals and contributing to the thriving small business community in Florida.

We wish you great success in your small business endeavors, and may your journey be filled with growth, prosperity, and fulfillment.

Epilogue:

Final Thoughts From The Author

As we conclude this journey through "The Florida Small Business Legal Handbook: Starting and Operating a Business," we reflect on the knowledge and insights shared in this comprehensive guide. We hope that the information provided has served as a valuable resource, empowering you to navigate the intricacies of starting and running a small business in Florida.

Building and growing a business is a dynamic and ever-evolving process. The landscape of business and entrepreneurship continues to evolve, influenced by technological advancements, economic trends, and societal changes. Therefore, it is essential to stay informed, adapt to new challenges, and embrace opportunities that arise.

Remember, the journey of entrepreneurship is not without its ups and downs. Challenges will inevitably arise, but it is how we respond to them that defines our success. Embrace a growth mindset, view setbacks as learning experiences, and seek innovative solutions to overcome obstacles.

In addition to the knowledge gained from this handbook, remember the value of collaboration and seeking support from others. Engage with local chambers of commerce, business associations, and mentorship programs to tap into the wisdom and experiences of fellow entrepreneurs. Building a strong network and seeking guidance from professionals can provide valuable insights and support throughout your entrepreneurial journey.

As you embark on your small business venture in Florida, remember the significance of ethical practices and corporate social responsibility. By maintaining transparency, promoting fair employment practices, protecting customer privacy, and engaging in sustainable business operations, you contribute not only to your business's success but also to the well-being of the community and environment.

Keep in mind that this handbook serves as a guide and reference, but it is not exhaustive. Stay informed about legal and regulatory changes specific to Florida and your industry. Seek professional advice when needed, particularly from attorneys and consultants who specialize in small business matters. Continuously educate yourself and adapt your strategies to remain competitive and compliant.

Lastly, celebrate your achievements and milestones along the way. Acknowledge the hard work, dedication, and passion that you have poured into your business. Remember that success comes in different forms and at different paces. Stay true to your vision, remain resilient in the face of challenges, and continue to pursue your entrepreneurial dreams.

On behalf of the author, publisher, and all those involved in creating this handbook, we extend our sincere congratulations on your journey as a small business owner in Florida. May your business thrive, create meaningful impact, and bring fulfillment and prosperity to your life and the lives of those you serve.

Best wishes on your entrepreneurial endeavors,

Nikollasa Achli

Author - "The Florida Small Business Legal Handbook: Starting and Operating a Business"

www.ingramcontent.com/pod-product-compliance
Lightning Source LLC
Chambersburg PA
CBHW060829220526
45466CB00003B/1027